Archaeological Survey of India

A REPORT ON A TOUR OF EXPLORATION OF THE ANTIQUITIES IN THE TARAI, NEPAL

THE REGION OF KAPILAVASTU;

DURING

FEBRUARY AND MARCH, 1899.

ILLUSTRATED BY 32 PLATES,

BY

BABU PURNA CHANDRA MUKHERJI,

LATELY EMPLOYED ON ARCHAEOLOGICAL EXPLORATIONS UNDER THE GOVERNMENT OF THE NORTH-WESTERN PROVINCES AND OUDH.

WITH A PREFATORY NOTE

BY

MR. VINCENT A. SMITH, B.A.
M.R.A.S., M.A.S.B., M.N.S.L., F.A.U.,
(TRINITY COLLEGE, DUBLIN)

No. XXVI, Part I of the Imperial Series

GYAN

Published by

GYAN

Gyan Publishing House
5, Ansari Road
Daryaganj, New Delhi-110002
Phone: 011-47034999, 9811692060
E-mail: books@gyanbooks.com

Distribution Network
gyanbooks.com
India, USA, Canada, UK, Australia, France

ISBN : 978-81-212-2422-2 (HB)
First Published, 1901

2nd Impression 2021

Printed at: Gyan Press, Delhi.

A Report on a Tour of Exploration of the Antiquities in the Tarai, Nepal
Author: Babu Purna Chandra MukherJi

Archæological Survey of India.

A REPORT ON A TOUR OF EXPLORATION

OF THE

ANTIQUITIES IN THE TARAI, NEPAL

THE REGION OF KAPILAVASTU;

DURING

FEBRUARY AND MARCH, 1899.

ILLUSTRATED BY 32 PLATES,

BY

BABU PURNA CHANDRA MUKHERJI,
LATELY EMPLOYED ON ARCHÆOLOGICAL EXPLORATIONS UNDER THE GOVERNMENT OF THE NORTH-WESTERN PROVINCES AND OUDH.

WITH A PREFATORY NOTE

BY

MR. VINCENT A. SMITH, B.A.,
M.R.A.S., M.A.S.B., M.N.S.L., F.A.U., (TRINITY COLLEGE, DUBLIN).

No. XXVI, PART I, OF THE IMPERIAL SERIES.

CALCUTTA:
OFFICE OF THE SUPERINTENDENT OF GOVERNMENT PRINTING, INDIA.
1901.

List of Volumes constituting the new Imperial series of the Reports of the Archæological Survey of India.

Prescribed number in new series.	Name of book.	Author or Editor.	Date (passed or proposed) of publication.	Provincial number. Western India.	Southern India.	Northern India.
I	Report of the first season's operations in the Belgaum and Kaladgi Districts.	Burgess	1874	I	...	...
II	Report on the Antiquities of Kathiawar and Kach	Ditto	1876	II	...	...
III	Report on the Antiquities of the Bidar and Aurangabad Districts.	Ditto	1878	III	...	...
IV	The Buddhist caves and their inscriptions	Ditto	1883	IV	...	...
V	The caves of Elura and the other Brahmanical and Jaina caves in Western India.	Ditto	1884	V	...	...
VI	The Buddhist Stupas of Amravati and Jaggayyapeta	Ditto	1887	...	I	...
VII	Lists of Antiquarian Remains in the Presidency of Madras (Volume I).	Sewell	1882	...	II	...
VIII	Lists of Inscriptions and sketch of Dynasties of Southern India (Volume II).	Ditto	1884	...	III	...
IX	South Indian Inscriptions (Volume I)	Hultzsch	1890	...	IV	...
X	Ditto ditto (Volume II)	Ditto	1891	...	V	...
XI	Report on the Sharqi Architecture of Jaunpur	Führer and Smith	1889	...	...	I
XII	Monumental Antiquities and Inscriptions in the North-Western Provinces and Oudh.	Führer	1891	...	...	II
XIII	Epigraphia Indica of the Archæological Survey of India (Volume I).	Burgess	1891	...	...	...
XIV	Epigraphia Indica of the Archæological Survey of India (Volume II).	Ditto	1893	...	...	...
XV	South Indian Buddhist antiquities	Rea	1894	...	VI	...
XVI	Revised List of Antiquities, Bombay	Cousens	1897	VIII	...	...
XVII	List of Architectural and Archæological Remains in Coorg	Rea	1894	...	VII	...
XVIII	Report on the Moghal Architecture of Fatehpur-Sikri	Smith	1895	...	...	III
XIX	List of Monumental Antiquities and Inscriptions in the Central Provinces and Berar.	Cousens	1897	...	...	IV
XX	The Jaina Stupa and some other Antiquities of Mathura	Smith, V. A.	1900	...	...	V
XXI	Chalukyan Architecture including examples from the Ballari District in Madras.	Rea	1896	...	VIII	...
XXII	Bower manuscripts	Hœrnle	1894	...	...	...
XXIII	Muhammadan Architecture in Gujarat	Burgess	1896	VI	...	...
XXIV	The Muhammadan Architecture of Ahmedabad	Ditto	...	VII	...	...
XXV	Monumental Remains of the Dutch East India Company in the Presidency of Madras.	Rea	1897	...	IX	...
XXVI	Report on results of explorations in the Nepal Tarai, Part I	Mukherji	1901	...	...	VI
XXVII	The Monumental Antiquities and Inscriptions in Rajputana and Central India.	Führer	1898	...	...	VII
XXVIII	The Monumental Antiquities and Inscriptions in the Punjab	Ditto	1898	...	...	VIII
XXIX	South Indian Inscriptions, Volume III, Part I	Hultzsch	1899	...	X	...
XXX	Moghul Colour Decoration of Agra	Smith	1899	...	...	IX
XXXI	List of Antiquarian Remains in His Highness the Nizam's Territory.	Cousens	1900	...	...	...

PREFATORY NOTE.

BY

VINCENT A. SMITH, ESQ., B.A., M.R.A.S., M.A.S.B., M.N.S.L., F.A.U., (TRINITY COLLEGE, DUBLIN), OF THE INDIAN CIVIL SERVICE.

IN accordance with the request of the Government of India I prefix a note of explanation and comment to Mr. Mukherji's Report on his explorations in the Nepalese Tarai.

Major Waddell, I.M.S.

I had hoped to be able to discuss also the report which Major Waddell had promised to submit, but unfortunately no report from him has been received.

Instructions given to Mr. Mukherji.

Before examining the results attained by Mr. Mukherji it will be convenient to reproduce the instructions which were given to him by me at the request of the Government of the North-Western Provinces and Oudh.

INSTRUCTIONS.

(1) The explorer should first try and fix the position of the city of Kapilavastu, as a whole, as accurately as possible, in relation to points within British territory, to Taulivâ, Niglivâ, and the great mounds at Tilaurâ-Kot, Lori-kî-kudân, and the various Thâru villages.

The outline of the city should then be plotted on a map, and endeavours made to ascertain the position of the gates. Several of Hiuen Tsiang's notes of position are with reference to the gates.

(2). The position of the *stupas* of Krakuchandra and of Koṇagamanâ should be determined with reference to the city, and mapped so far as practicable. If the explorer succeeds in doing these things, he will probably be able to fix with approximate certainty the position of many of the monuments mentioned by Hiuen Tsiang, and he can then proceed to verify or disprove his conclusions by excavations at carefully selected points.

(3) Photographs should be freely taken, and if any inscriptions are found, *mechanical* facsimiles of them should be at once prepared. Inscriptions, the existence of which is not verified by facsimiles, cannot be accepted.

(4) The Nepalese will not allow any objects found to be removed, but they make no difficulty about drawing or photographing them. Any observations taken to verify the geographical position of the city by observations will need to be conducted with discretion, as the Nepalese authorities are jealous of surveys.

(5) The explorer ought to have several copies of sheet No. 188 of the North-Western Provinces and Oudh Survey (one inch to the mile), on which Birdpur House is marked, and should extend that sheet to the best of his ability so as to cover the ruins.

(6) Dr. Führer has attempted to do this, but, as I have shown, without much success. Very careful and minute notes of all localities explored should be kept systematically in note books written up at the time, which should be worked up afterwards.

Ground plans of all buildings examined should be made. So far as possible, a rough plan should be constructed showing the distribution of the ruins, and the relative positions of the principal masses.

(7) I may add that Dr. Führer's notes on the Piprâvâ *stupa* in his Progress Report are very inaccurate. The correct figures are given in the paper entitled "The Piprâhwâ *stupa*, containing Relics of Buddha," by William Claxton Peppé, Esq., communicated with a Note by Vincent A. Smith, I.C.S., M.R.A.S. (*Journal, Royal Asiatic Society*, July, 1898.)

The Map.

The difficulties of the exploration have been briefly stated in the Report, and, considering the obstacles in his way and the shortness of the time available, I think that Mr. Mukherji did very well. His map (Plate I) is quite accurate enough for all practical purposes, and is of great value. Most of the region investigated is open country where the traveller when riding an elephant can see round him for miles. The limits of the forest are shown on the map. I have visited more than once several of the sites described and am thus able to guarantee the general accuracy of Mr. Mukherji's work.

Mr. Mukherji's chronological theories.

Since my retirement I have had leisure to examine Mr. Mukherji's chronological theories (page 16), which he has developed in a pamphlet entitled "The Indian Chronology, Buddhistic Period," Lucknow, 1899. This little work has been sympathetically reviewed by Professor Rhys Davids in the Journal of the Royal Asiatic Society for July 1900, and thus introduced to the consideration of scholars. One of the fundamental propositions of the author's system is the assignment of the different classes of the "Asoka Edicts" to different kings. Mr. Mukherji assigns to one sovereign the Seven Pillar Edicts found at Delhi and elsewhere, and to another and later sovereign the Fourteen Rock Edicts.

Priyadarsi and Asoka are identical.

A minute and impartial examination of the whole of the Asoka (Priyadarsi) inscriptions of all classes has convinced me that Mr. Mukherji's theory is utterly untenable, and that the evidence in favour of the unity of authorship of *all* the Priyadarsi inscriptions is conclusive. I am equally convinced that the commonly accepted identification of King Priyadarsi with the Maurya emperor Asoka is certainly right and remains unshaken.

Chronology of reign of Asoka.

Sir Alexander Cunningham's dates (B.C. 259—222) for Asoka are too late. M. Senart, I think, has made the nearest approach to the truth of the Mauryan chronology. I closely follow him in fixing (with certain additions) the leading dates of Asoka's reign approximately as follows:—

B. C.	272	Accession.
„	269	Solemn coronation (*abhisheka*).
„	261	Conquest of Kalinga—and imperfect conversion to Buddhism.
„	257	Earliest rock inscriptions.
„	256	Publication of the series of Fourteen Rock Edicts.
„	255	Enlargement for second time of the *stupa* of Kanakamuni.
„	250	Dedication of No. III cave at Barâbar near Gayâ.
„	249	Religious tour in Nepalese Tarai, visit to the *stûpa* of Kanaka-muni, and erection of Niglivâ and Rummin-dei pillars.
„	243	Pillar Edicts Nos. I—VI.
„	242	Publication of the series of Seven Pillar Edicts, complete.
„	232	Death.

Mr. Mukherji's date B.C. 441 for the Niglivâ and Rummin-dei Pillars is impossible. The statement of the reasons for these conclusions would require more space than is available in this Note, and will be found in articles which will appear in the Journal of the Royal Asiatic Society for July and October, 1901.[1]

Value of the Tarai pillar inscriptions.

The inscriptions on these two pillars, brief though they are, make valuable additions to the history both of Buddhism and of Asoka. They prove, among other things, that the veneration of the Buddhas previous to Gautama was already well established in

[1] The Tarai Pillar inscriptions have been edited and translated by Bühler in *Epigraphia Indica*, V, 1. But *vigaḍabhi* is to be translated "a horse" and not "a big sun." Kanakamuni, Koṇagamanâ, and Koṇâkamana are variant forms of one name. The articles referred to are entitled "The Unity of Authorship of the Priyadarsi Inscriptions", and "The Identity of Priyadarsi with Asoka Maurya, and some connected problems."

the middle of the third century B.C., that Asoka was a zealous Buddhist in 249 B.C., and that the Nepalese Tarai was included in his vast empire.

Antiquities at Sâgarwâ.

The meagre genuine results of Dr. Führer's excavations at Sâgarwâ are set forth in pages 25—28 of Mr. Mukherji's report, and are fully illustrated in plates VIII to XIII. Attention is invited to the remarkable plan of the foundations of the large building which was destroyed by the excavations of the Nepalese and Dr. Führer. (Plates IX, X.)

The bricks (Plates XI, XI*a*, XII, and XII*a*) under which the caskets in the *stupas* were deposited are extremely curious, and offer an interesting series of pictures of ancient Indian weapons.

Square *stupas*.

Mr. Mukherji correctly observes (page 26) that the fact that the basements of the small *stupas* were square does not prove that the *stupas* themselves were square. Mr. William Peppé and I happened to ride up on the 28th January 1898 just as Dr. Führer was exhuming the deposit of five caskets from *stupa* No. 5, and I remember that Dr. Führer specially drew our attention to the occurrence of square *stupas* as a remarkable novelty. Unfortunately no drawings of sections of the *stupas* were made to verify the observation, but my impression is that the buildings were really square. With reference to this subject the following passage is relevant.

"Then the Buddha himself erected (or, himself caused to appear) a Stupa of Kasyapa Buddha, its foundation four-square, surrounded by an ornamental railing, in the middle of it a four-cornered double-staged plinth, above which rose a lofty staff with a circular ball (or, with circular rings).

Then Buddha, said: 'Let all Stupas be fashioned in this way. This is the model of the old towers of the ancient Buddhas,' etc."

The book proceeds to give an account of the accessories of a *stupa*, lakes, railings, niches, etc.[1]

Alleged *stûpa* of Koṇagamanâ does not exist.

Mr. Mukherji's remark (page 30) that the alleged *stupa* of Koṇagamanâ "is not in existence," is, I am sorry to say, quite true. I have myself visited the spot and failed to see the building, which was carefully searched for in vain by Major Waddell and Dr. Hoey, as well as by Mr. Mukherji. Dr. Führer's account of this imaginary building was as follows:—

"The great Nirvâna-*stupa* of Koṇagamanâ, or Koṇâkamana, is, despite its great age, still fairly well-preserved, and rears its imposing pile close to Asoka's Edict Pillar, just one mile and a half due north-east of Tilaurâ-Koṭ and about one mile south of the village of Niglivâ . . . . Amongst the heaps of ruins, the Nirvâṇa-stupa of Koṇagamanâ is clearly discernible, the base of its hemispherical dome being about 101 feet in diameter, and its present height still about thirty feet. The dome seems to have been constructed of solid brick to a depth of about 20 feet, whilst the interior is filled up with earth-packing. This dome rests on a great circular mass, 109 feet in diameter, built in the shape of a huge brick drum, about six feet high, cased with solid bricks, the bricks used being of very great size, 16 inches by 11 by 3, thus leaving a procession path round the exterior of about eight feet in breadth. About 10 feet beyond the great circular base all round

[1] From "Laws respecting the erection of stupas" in the 33rd *kiouen* of the Mahâsanghika copy of the Vinaya, translated by Beal in "Remarks on the Bharhut Sculptures and Inscriptions," *Ind. Ant.* volume XI (Feb. 1882), page 47.

was apparently a stone-railing with gateways, the positions of which can still be traced. It is thus abundantly evident that the corporeal relics of Koṇagamanâ, collected from his funeral pyre, were carefully and securely interred in this stupa, and that his Nirvâṇa stupa is undoubtedly one of the oldest Buddhist monuments still existing in India. On all sides around this interesting monument are ruined monasteries, fallen columns, and broken sculptures."

This elaborate description was not supported by a single drawing, plan, or photograph. Every word of it is false. The stone-railing, the fallen columns, and the broken sculptures had no existence save in Dr. Führer's fertile imagination. ("Monograph on Buddha Sakyamuni's Birth-Place in the Nepalese Tarai," by A. Führer, Ph.D., Archæological Surveyor, North-Western Provinces and Oudh, Allahabad, 1897, pages 22, 124. This work has been withdrawn from circulation by the Government of India).[1] The large so-called "*stupa-vihâra*" at Sâgarwâ was really about 100 feet in length, and was the only large building excavated by Dr. Führer.

The Nigâli Sâgar pillar is not *in situ*.

Equally imaginative are the details given by Dr. Führer concerning his alleged excavation of the base of the broken Asoka pillar lying at the Nigâli Sâgar. He writes:—

"The lower inscribed portion of this pillar (Plate IV), which on excavation was found to measure 10 feet 6 inches in depth, and at its base 8 feet 2 inches in circumference, is still fixed *in situ*, resting on a square masonry foundation, 7 feet by 7 by 1, and being imbedded in the western embankment of the lake. A short distance to the north-east, close to the brink of the water, lies the upper half of Asoka's Edict Pillar (see Plate V), measuring 14 feet 9 inches in length, and 2 feet in diameter at its uppermost and 2 feet 6 inches at its lowest end. The lion capital is wanting."[2]

Mr. Mukherji writes:—"The pillar is not *in situ;* for Dr. Führer was mistaken in saying so. When Major Waddell excavated below, the broken bottom was exposed, when no foundation or basement was discovered," (page 30). Dr. Hoey was with Major Waddell during this operation, and a photograph was taken. It is impossible that Dr. Führer should have been mistaken, inasmuch as he gives the dimensions of the imaginary foundation.

Other forgeries of Dr. Führer.

These fictions about the Koṇagamanâ *stupa* and pillar do not stand alone. The inscriptions of the Sâkyas alleged to have been found in the small *stupas* at Sâgarwâ are impudent forgeries,[3] and when Dr. Führer supplied the Burmese priest U Ma with sham relics of Buddha, he endeavoured to support the imposition by a forged inscription of Upagupta, the *guru* of Asoka. In the course of my official duty the whole case was investigated by me, and no doubt as to the facts is possible. I find that the reserved language used in previous official documents has been sometimes misinterpreted, and it is now necessary in the interests of truth to speak out plainly.

Original position of the Nigâli Sâgar pillar.

In a subsequent part of this essay reasons will be given for believing that the pillar lying at the Nigâlî Sâgar has been moved about eight or thirteen miles from its original position which was probably either at Sisaniâ or at Paltâ Devî. It is impossible

---

[1] The phrase "ruined monasteries, fallen columns, and broken sculptures" is stolen from the "ruined temples, fallen columns, and broken sculptures" of Cunningham's "Bhilsa Topes," page 183. The imaginary description of the Koṇagamanâ *stupa* is taken from page 321 of the same work, where the Tope of Satdhâra is described in words practically identical with those used by Dr. Führer:—"The base of the dome is 101 feet in diameter; but its present height is only 30 feet."

[2] "Monograph," page 22. These also were suggested by the ink inscriptions found on the caskets of the Bhilsa topes (Cunningham, page 350).

[3] Dr. Führer's "Progress Report" for 1897-98, and my "Progress Report" for 1898-99.

that Koṇagamanâ's *stupa* should have stood anywhere near Niglivâ. The belief that it ought to have been found near that village was so strongly held by Dr. Führer that it induced him to invent the *stupa* which he could not discover; and to place at the basis of the pillar a foundation " of imagination all compact."

Asoka pillar at Guṭivâ.

The discovery of a broken Asoka pillar at Guṭivâ is of importance. The details given at page 31 of the report prove conclusively that this pillar is in its original position. The few lines devoted to Guṭivâ by Dr. Führer are full of misstatements.

Tilaurâ-Koṭ and Chitrâdei.

Dr. Führer identified Tilaurâ-Koṭ (*Monograph*, page 22) with the town where Kanakamuni (Koṇagamanâ) Buddha was born, but did not describe the remains. Tilaurâ-Koṭ is certainly the ruins of a walled town. Chitrâdei, on the opposite, or western bank, of the river Bângangâ, seems also to have been a place of some importance. Mr. Mukherji's description of Tilaurâ-Koṭ and Chitrâdei (pages 19—25, Plates II to VII) is of interest and value. In January 1900, I visited Tilaurâ-Koṭ with Professor Rhys Davids and Mr. George Peppé.

Remains north and north-west of Chitrâdei.

The report (page 25) that undescribed ancient remains exist hidden in the forest ten or twelve miles north and north-west of Chitrâdei at places called Sobangaṛh and Changât is worthy of verification or disproof.

Discoveries at Rummindei.

Mr. Mukherji's researches at Rummindei, the site of the Lumbini Garden, produced results of great interest, and it is much to be regretted that the time at his disposal did not permit of more thorough excavation. The buried temple, portions of the plinth of which are illustrated in Plates XXI and XXII, was evidently a fine building. Systematic and complete excavation would no doubt disclose the eight *stupas* enumerated by Hiuen Tsiang, which were evidently all comprised within the limits of the existing mound of ruins.

The Nativity group.

Mr. Mukherji was fortunate enough to secure photographs and a drawing of the Nativity group of sculpture enshrined in the little modern temple which marks the site of the tree of the nativity. This group was first seen and recognized by Dr. Hoey. I was not admitted to the shrine at either of my visits. Mr. Mukherji took photographs of the group both with and without the head of Mâyâ, which he recovered outside the shrine, but the work is so much defaced and besmeared that no photograph can come out very clearly. Plate XXIV*a* has therefore been prepared from a drawing in preference to the photographs.

The composition of the group differs from that in any other known example of this favourite subject of Buddhist art. The ordinary type is thus described by Dr. Burgess :—

" A favourite subject in all Buddhist art and legend is the birth of Siddhârtha, the 'Sâkya Muni,' in the Lumbini Garden. The variations in the treatment are trifling. His mother Mâyâ stands under the *plaksha* tree;[1] her sister Prajâpati at her left side supports her, while the other women behind are in attendance, and gods above shower down flowers or rejoice at the event. The child

[1] The various legends differ as to the particular tree.

springs from his mother's right side. Śakra or Indra receives the infant on a fine Kâśika cloth, and Mahâbrahma and other superhuman beings attend."[1]

A fragmentary sculpture in the Calcutta Museum presents the scene in a manner closely resembling the Rummin-dei group. The fragment, which comes from Loriyân Tangai[2], shows the two gods, Śakra and Brahmâ, of whom one is receiving the child from its mother's side, and also shows the child after the birth standing on the ground, about to take the "seven steps" celebrated in legend. The figures to the left of Mâyâ are lost.[3] The Rummin-dei group agrees with the Loriyân Tangai fragment in representing both the delivery of the infant into the hands of the god, and also the child standing on the ground, but differs in introducing Prajâpati on the proper right of Mâyâ under whose uplifted arm she stands. The attitude of the foremost male figure shows that he is receiving the infant on a cloth, although the sculpture is so much damaged that the infant has disappeared. Probably this Rummin-dei group is the oldest known example of the nativity subject.

Certainty of identification of Rummin-dei with Lumbini garden.

The identity of Rummin-dei with the Lumbini garden of Buddhist tradition does not, as Mr. Mukherji observes, admit of doubt in the mind of any person who knows the facts. But, inasmuch as all my readers cannot be expected to be familiar with the details, it is advisable to re-state clearly the evidence which conclusively establishes the identity. That evidence falls under five principal heads; namely :—

(1) The name Rummin is practically identical with Lumbini, or Lummini, as it is written in the inscription, which is in the Magadhî language, in which medial or initial *r* of Sanskrit in always replaced by *l*;

(2) Hiuen Tsiang notes that the little river which flows past the garden to the south-east is locally called "the river of oil." ("à côté, il y a une petite rivière qui coule au sud-est. Les habitants du pays l'appellent la rivière d'huile." *Julien*, I, 325.) That little river is to this day the Tilâr Nadî (*tel*=oil);

(3) The bathing tank lay some 20 (Fa-hien), or 25 (Hiuen Tsiang), paces south of the nativity tree. The little shrine which contains the nativity group of sculpture is situated about 25 paces north of the pond, which still exists with clear water as described by the pilgrims;—

(4) Hiuen Tsiang records that close to the *stupas* marking the spot where the gods received the infant Bodhisattva, then was a great stone pillar crowned by the image of a horse, which had been erected by Asoka. In the course of time this pillar had been struck by lightning, and at the time of the pilgrim's visit, it lay on the ground, split in the middle.[4]

The undisturbed pillar, with a perfectly preserved inscription of Priyadarsi (Aśoka) now stands close to the nativity temple, and it is split down the middle,

---

[1] "The Gandhâra Sculptures," by James Burgess, C.I.E., LL.D., F.R.S.E., in "Journal of Indian Art and Industry" for July 1898, page 35. Plate 10, figure 1.

[2] Loriyân, or Lauriyân, is the name of the *tangai* or valley on the northern slope of the Shâhkoṭ pass which leads from the Yusufzai district into the south of Swât. Loriyân is near the north end of the Shâhkoṭ pass, some way to the south of the large village of Aladand and near the hamlet of Piyatâna. (Burgess, *op. cit.* for Jan. 1900, page 90.)

[3] This fragment is described and figured by Burgess (*op. cit.* for Jan. 1900, page 75).

[4] "À côté, et à une petite distance des *Stoûpas*, ... il y avait une grande colonne de pierre, au sommet de laquelle on avait sculpté un cheval. Elle avait été élevée par le roi *Wou-yeou* (Açôka). Dans la suite des temps, elle fut foudroyée par un méchant dragon. Cette colonne gît à terre, brisée par le milieu." (*Julien*, I, 324.) Julien's rendering of the passage is preferable to Beal's. Hiuen Tsiang's reference to the dragon is explained by the Taouist mythology so popular in China. "On the banks of rivers the shrines of dragon-kings are common. Any remarkable appearance in the sky or on the surface of the water is frequently pointed to as a dragon, or a phenomenon occasioned by the presence of a dragon. One of their divinities is called 'the Ruler of Thunder' and another 'the mother of Lightning'." (Edkins, "Religion in China," fourth edition, page 105.)

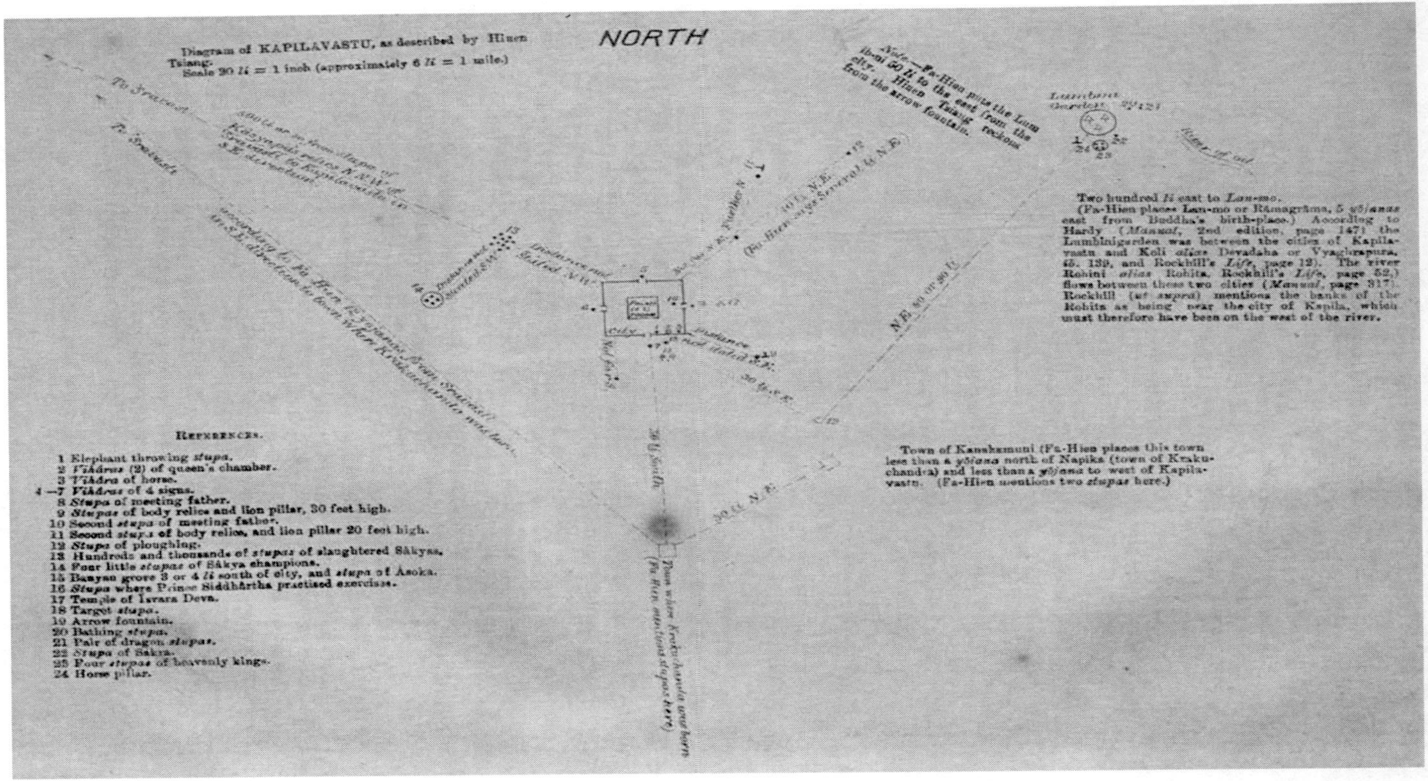

NORTH
Diagram of KAPILAVASTU, as described by Hiuen Tsiang.
Scale 30 li = 1 inch (approximately 6 li = 1 mile.)
To Śrâvastî
To Śrâvastî
Note.—Fa-Hien puts the Lum-bini 50 li to the east from the city. Hiuen Tsiang reckons from the arrow fountain.
Lumbini Garden
Two hundred li east to Lan-mo.
(Fa-Hien places Lan-mo or Râmagrâma, 5 yôjanas east from Buddha's birth-place.) According to Hardy (Manual, 2nd edition, page 147) the Lumbinigarden was between the cities of Kapilavastu and Koli alias Devadaha or Vyaghrapura, ib. 139, and Rockhill's Life, page 12). The river Rohini alias Rohita, Rockhill's Life, page 52,) flows between these two cities (Manual, page 317). Rockhill (ut supra) mentions the banks of the Rohita as being near the city of Kapila, which must therefore have been on the west of the river.
N.E. 80 or 90 li
30 li N.E.
30 li S.E.
30 li South
Not far S.
Town where Krakuchanda was born (Fa-Hien mentions stupas here)
Town of Kanakamuni (Fa-Hien places this town less than a yôjana north of Napika (town of Krakuchanda) and less than a yôjana to west of Kapilavastu. (Fa-Hien mentions two stupas here.)
according to Fa-Hien 12 yojanas from Śrâvastî in S.E. direction to town where Krakuchanda was born.
REFERENCES.
1 Elephant throwing stupa.
2 Vihâras (2) of queen's chamber.
3 Vihâra of horse.
4—7 Vihâras of 4 signs.
8 Stupa of meeting father.
9 Stupas of body relics and lion pillar, 30 feet high.
10 Second stupa of meeting father.
11 Second stupa of body relics, and lion pillar 20 feet high.
12 Stupa of ploughing.
13 Hundreds and thousands of stupas of slaughtered Sâkyas.
14 Four little stupas of Sâkya champions.
15 Banyan grove 3 or 4 li south of city, and stupa of Asoka.
16 Stupa where Prince Siddhârtha practised exercises.
17 Temple of Isvara Deva.
18 Target stupa.
19 Arrow fountain.
20 Bathing stupa.
21 Pair of dragon stupas.
22 Stupa of Sakra.
23 Four stupas of heavenly kings.
24 Horse pillar.

apparently by lightning. The inscription mentions that the column had been surmounted by a horse (*vigaḍabhi*), and expressly states that "Here was Buddha born." The brick railing which now surrounds the base of the pillar is built of small bricks and is evidently of comparatively modern date. The pillar, which was prostrate in the seventh century, may have been set up again by one of the Buddhist Pâla kings in the eleventh or twelfth century;

(5) The existence of the nativity group of sculpture in the position assigned by tradition to the nativity tree.

The site of the Lumbini garden is therefore fixed with absolute certainty. We know from the testimony of both the Chinese pilgrims that Kapilavastu, the city of the father of Gautama Buddha, was from 9 to 16 miles distant from the Lumbini garden, in a westerly direction.

Difficulty of identifying Kapilavastu.

Apparently nothing should be easier than to fix the exact position of the city, and to locate its principal monuments. As a matter of fact, the problem presents very serious difficulties, and its solution is far from obvious.

The indications of the position of Kapilavastu given in the Buddhist sacred books are too vague to be of much use. The only serviceable guides are the Chinese pilgrims, Fa-hien and Hiuen Tsiang, both of whom give bearings and distances which appear to be very precise, and yet are on the face of them inconsistent.

Before discussing the question of the exact site of Kapilavastu I will re-state in a convenient form the principal indications given by the pilgrims.

I. Relative position of Srâvasti.

Fâ-hien says that the distance from Srâvasti in a south-easterly direction to Na-pei-kea, the birth place of Krakuchandra Buddha was 12 *yojanas;* from Na-pei-kea the distance northwards to the birth place of Koṇagamanâ was less than a *yojana*, and from the birth place of Koṇagamanâ eastward to Kapilavastu was likewise less than a *yojana*. Kapilavastu would therefore lie about 12½ or 13 *yojanas* in a south-easterly direction from Srâva ti. That distance is equivalent to about 90 to 100 miles. The city would have been some five or six miles distant from the town of Koṇâgamana, and not much farther from the town of Krakuchandra.

Position relative to Srâvasti.

Hiuen Tsiang gives the bearing of Kapilavastu south-east from the *stupa* of the body of Kâśyapa north of Srâvasti as "about 500" *li* (*environ cinq cents li*). The Kâśyapa *stupa* was evidently close to Srâvasti, so that the difference in starting point is slight. The *yojana* of the pilgrims comprised 40 *li*, and 500 *li*,=12½ *yojanas*. The distance and direction from Srâvasti to Kapilavastu, as given independently by both pilgrims, therefore, agree closely, and the statements of both pilgrims may be accepted as correct, to the effect that Kapilavastu lay ninety to a hundred miles distant from Srâvasti in a direction between south and east. The exact interpretation to be placed on this agreement in the pilgrims' statements will be discussed later.

Unfortunately, the bearing from Srâvasti is not of much use for determining the exact site of Kapilavastu, because the distance is so great that a certain margin must be allowed in the reduction of *lis* and *yojanas* to miles, and because a difference of opinion exists as to the position of Srâvasti. Personally, I have no doubt that the true site of the city

The true site of Srâvasti.

has been approximately fixed at the point where the Râptî issues from the hills north-east of Nepâlganj railway station. I venture to think that I have succeeded in demonstrating that Saheṭ-Maheṭ on the borders of the Gonḍâ and Bahraich districts in Oudh cannot possibly be Srâvasti.[1]

Dr. Führer substantially agrees.

Dr. Führer, from information independently supplied to him, arrived at practically the same conclusion, the only difference between us being that he places the city on the left, or eastern, bank of the Râptî, whereas the ruins seen by Dr. Vost and me are on the right, or western, bank. It is quite possible that extensive remains exist on both sides of the river in the dense forest. Dr. Führer wrote (*Monograph*, page 35, *note*):

"I have, however, reliable information to prove that the ruins of Srâvasti are to be found in the Nepâl Tarai, on the left bank of the Râptî, the ancient Achiravati, close to the modern village of Materiya, just 15 miles north-east of Chârdâ. The two monoliths of Asoka erected in front of the Jetavana monastery in Anathapiṇḍika's Park, are said to be still *in situ*, which information I hope to verify in the winter season of 1897-98."

The opportunity for verification never came. I shall not be surprised if the information given to Dr. Führer should prove to be correct. Materiya, the village in Nepalese territory mentioned by him, is not shown in the maps available to me.

II. Relative position of the towns of the previous Buddhas.

Position relative to the towns of the previous Buddhas.

In their statements as to the position of the town of Koṇagamanâ in relation to the town of Krakuchandra the two pilgrims substantially agree. The distance, 30 *li*, equivalent to three-quarters of a *yojana*, as stated by Hiuen Tsiang, is in exact agreement with the statement of Fa-hien that the interval between the town was "less than a *yojana*." Hiuen Tsiang is habitually (though not invariably) more precise in his definition of direction than his predecessor. The north-easterly bearing for the town of Koṇagamanâ given by Hiuen Tsiang may therefore be accepted as a more accurate version of the northerly bearing given by Fa-hien.

The result is that the town of Koṇagamanâ is fixed as lying five or six miles north-east of the town of Krakuchandra, which town, according to Hiuen Tsiang, lay 50 *li* or about 9 miles, south of Kapilavastu. The necessary inference is that Hiuen Tsiang places the town of Koṇagamanâ in a south-easterly direction from Kapilavastu at a distance of about five miles. Fa-hien, on the contrary, places Kapilavastu "less than a *yojana*," or five or six miles in an easterly direction from the town of Koṇagamanâ. All the versions of Fa-hien's travels agree in their rendering of the passage so that the hypothesis of error on the part of translators is inadmissible. The embarrassing discrepancy between the two travellers will be explained presently. Both writers are, I believe, correct in their statements.

III. Position of Kapilavastu relative to the Arrow-well and the Lumbini garden.

Position relative to the Arrow-well and Lumbini garden.

Hiuen Tsiang states that the Lumbini garden was 80 to 90 *li*, or about 15 miles, in a north-easterly direction from the Arrow-well, which was 30 *li* south-east from

[1] The question is fully discussed in my two essays entitled "Kausâmbî and Srâvasti" in *J. R. A. S.* for July 1898, page 503; and "Srâvasti," *ibid.* for January, 1900, page 1.

Kapilavastu. The necessary inference is that his Kapilavastu lay some 15 or 16 miles in a westerly direction from our fixed point the Lumbini garden.

Fa-hien, though mentioning that the Arrow-well was 30 *li* south-east of Kapilavastu, does not take bearings from the well. He travelled through the town of Koṇagamanâ some five miles eastward to Kapilavastu, and thence 50 *li*, or some 9 miles eastward, to the fixed point the Lumbini garden.

Taking that fixed point as a basis the two pilgrims give the following results, either as direct statements, or as necessary inferences :—

From	*To*	*Fa-hien*	*Hiuen Tsiang*
Lumbini garden	Krakuchandra T.	about south-west, about 13 or 14 miles (9+5 or 4 diagonal).	about 15 miles, nearly south-west.
Ditto	Koṇagamanâ T.	about west, 13 or 14 miles (9 + 4 or 5).	about the same as Fa-hien.[1]
Ditto	Arrow-well	about 8 or 9 miles, south-west.	80 or 90 *li*, about 15 miles, south-west.
Ditto	Kapilavastu	50 *li* or 9 miles, west.	15 or 16 miles, nearly the same as to the Arrow-well, but in westerly direction.

Points of difference and agreement.

The result is that the two pilgrims differ materially as to the position of Kapilavastu both with reference to the towns of the previous Buddhas, and with reference to the Lumbini garden. Hiuen Tsiang places Kapilavastu north of Krakuchandra's town, north-west of Koṇagamanâ's town, and some 15 or 16 miles in a westerly direction from the Lumbini garden. Fa-hien places Kapilavastu east of Koṇagamanâ's town, north-east of Krakuchandra's town and only 9 miles west from the Lumbini garden. The differences cannot be explained otherwise than in one of two ways, either by an error in the figures, or by the admission that the Kapilavastu visited by Hiuen Tsiang was a different place from that visited by Fa-hien. There is no doubt that the Lumbini garden visited by both pilgrims was the one. It will be observed that the distances and bearings from the fixed point, the Lumbini garden, to the towns of the previous Buddhas substantially agree. There is therefore a high probability that both pilgrims identified the same places as the towns of the previous Buddhas. The substantial agreement of the pilgrims' statements regarding the relative position of the fixed point and the towns of the previous Buddhas raises a presumption that the figures are right. That presumption becomes immensely strengthened if it can be shown that suitable sites for the two towns can be pointed out in the required directions and at the right distances from the Lumbini garden. Such sites can be indicated. On general principles of criticism, too, we are not entitled to pronounce our texts corrupt, or primary authorities mistaken, until the reality of the corruption or the error is proved by means of ascertained truths, not merely by guesses or hypotheses.

[1] Taking Rummin-dei as a centre, the Kapilavastu of Hiuen Tsiang and a place 9 miles south of it will fall on the same arc, the length of the radius of which according to Hiuen Tsiang's figures is about 15 miles. The distance of Koṇagamanâ's town according to Hiuen Tsiang is deduced from that of Krakuchandra's town, and, according to Fa-hien, may be deduced from that of Kapilavastu.

The Lumbini garden a fixed point.

Remembering that the ascertained identity of Rummin-dei and the Lumbini garden gives an absolutely fixed starting point, and that all the evidence shows that the Kapilavastu visited by the Chinese pilgrims was situated not many miles in a westerly direction from that fixed point, I proceed to discuss in the light of the actual existing facts the calculations and inferences examined in the preceding pages.

The country shown in Mr. Mukherji's map is for the most part open. It has been thoroughly traversed by several independent observers, and the positions of all ancient remains on the surface of any importance are known. The bearings and distances in the map are approximately correct, though they may in some cases err to the extent of a mile or two, at the most.

The 9-mile arc intersects Piprâvâ.

Let the reader now take a pair of compasses with Rummin-dei as a centre and describe to the west an arc with 9 miles (or 50 *li*) radius. That arc will cut the group of ruins near Piprâvâ and will not intersect any other ruins. *Primâ facie*, therefore, Piprâvâ is the Kapilavastu of Fa-hien. If this identification be assumed, Sisaniâ Pâṇre, some four or five miles in a north-westerly direction from Piprâvâ, corresponds well to Koṇagamanâ's town,[1] and Paltâ Devî, 5 miles south-west of Sisaniâ, is exactly in the position where Krakuchandra's town should be.

The 14-mile arc intersects Tilaurâ-Koṭ.

If the reader again takes up the compasses, and in accordance with Hiuen Tsiang's indication, describes an arc on the map of 14 miles radius (=15 or 16 by road), he will find that the arc cuts through Tilaurâ-Koṭ, which is the central part of a great mass of ruins extending for miles. *Primâ facie*, then, the Tilaurâ-Koṭ group of ruins is the Kapilavastu of Hiuen Tsiang.

Paltâ Devî-Krakuchandra's town.

The southern edge of this group of ruins is at or near Lori-kî-kudân, and measuring thence southward 50 *li*, or nine miles, according to Hiuen Tsiang's directions, we reach Paltâ Devî as representing Krakuchandra's town.

Thus the identity of Paltâ Devî with Krakuchandra's town is deduced from the measurements of Fa-hien on the assumption that Piprâvâ=Kapilavastu, and from the measurements of Hiuen Tsiang on the assumption that the Tilaurâ-Koṭ group=Kapilavastu. I have already shown independently that both pilgrims probably identified the same places as the towns of Krakuchandra and Koṇagamanâ respectively. That probability may now be considered a certainty, and the identification of Paltâ Devî with Krakuchandra's town becomes highly probable.

Piprâvâ = Kapilavastu of Fa-hien; Tilaurâ-Koṭ = Kapilavastu of Hiuen Tsiang.

I spent many hours in the vain attempt to harmonize the statements of Fa-hien and Hiuen Tsiang on the assumption, which I had never doubted, that they both described the same place as being Kapilavastu. At last a process of reasoning such as I have sketched above suddenly brought me to the unexpected conclusion that **Piprâvâ is the Kapilavastu of Fa-hien, whereas the city round Tilaurâ-Koṭ is the Kapilavastu of Hiuen Tsiang.**

The moment that this explanation flashed on my mind, all difficulties in the interpretation of the documents vanished. Each locality described dropped into its

[1] The map rather understates the distance, I think. I have been over the ground.

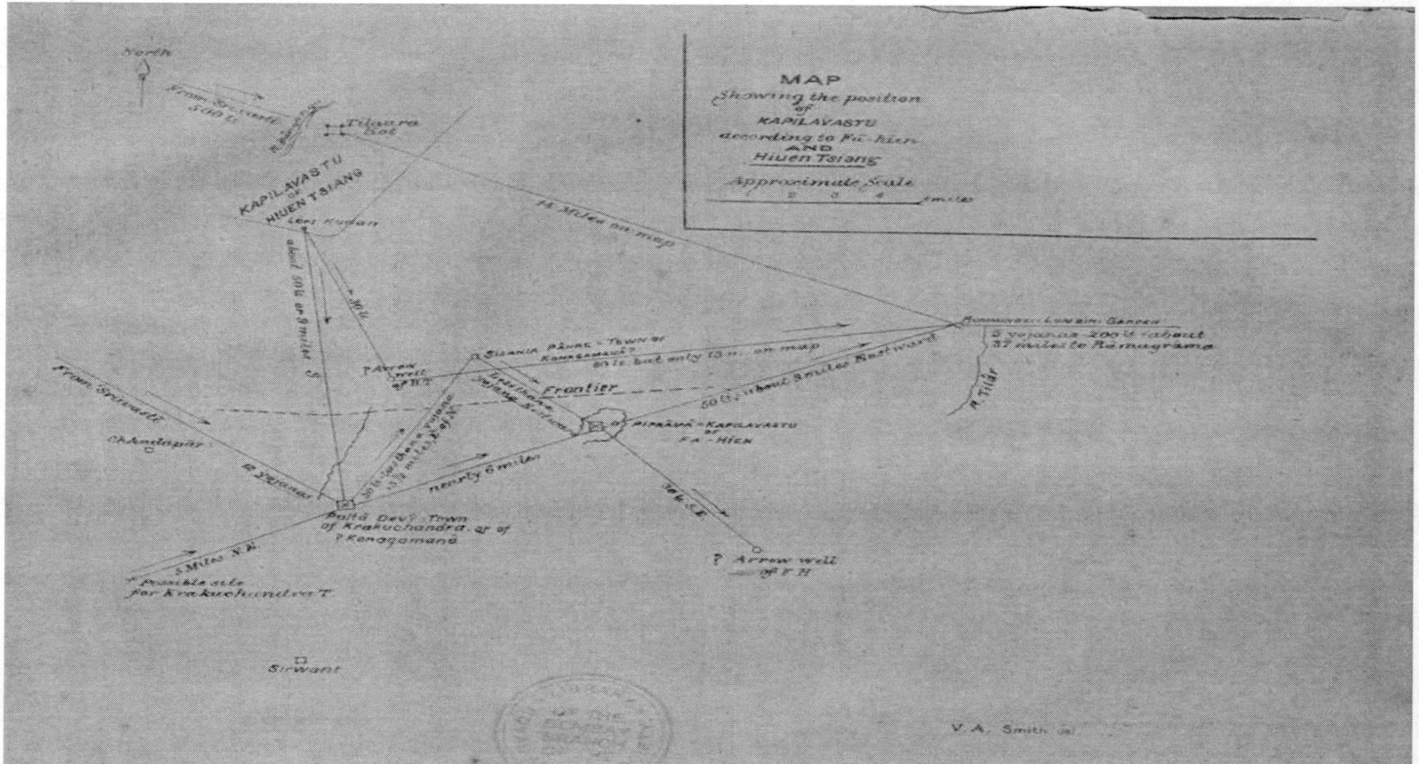
MAP
Showing the position
of
KAPILAVASTU
according to Fa-hian
AND
Hiuen Tsiang
Approximate Scale
North
Tilaura
Kot
KAPILAVASTU
of
HIUEN TSIANG
14 Miles on map
5 yojanas-200 li = about
37 miles to Rāmagrāma
R. Tilār
Frontier
From Srāvasti
Chhandapār
nearly 6 miles
? Arrow well
of F. H.
Possible site
for Krakuchandra T.
5 Miles N.W.
of Krakuchandra, or of
? Kanagamana
Sirwant
V. A. Smith del.

proper position in the itinerary of each pilgrim, and each itinerary fitted into the other. Hiuen Tsiang now supports Fa-hien, and Fa-hien supports Hiuen Tsiang.

Explanation of itinerary from Srâvasti.

The different methods in which the two pilgrims describe the approach to Kapilavastu from Srâvasti now become intelligible. The later traveller started from the *stupa* of Kâśyapa north of Srâvasti and made his way direct to the ruined city on the Bânganga. Doubtless he travelled along the road which still exists skirting the foot of the hills through Tulśipur and Panchpirwâ in the Gondâ District. His predecessor would have followed the same road for most of the way, but in the final stages he must have diverged to the south, and marched direct to Paltâ Devî, or Krakuchandra's town, to which he reckons the distance to be twelve *yojanas*. Fa-hien then moved on five miles to the north-east (he calls it north), and reached Sisaniâ, from which he marched five miles to the south-east (he calls it east), and so arrived at Piprâvâ, or Kapilavastu, from which the Lumbini garden was distant nine or ten miles. In recording the bearings of Kapilavastu and the Lumbini garden, Fa-hien, in accordance with his usual practice, simply notes the general easterly direction of his march, and disregards minor details. He found Koṇagamanâ's town more or less directly on the road from Krakuchandra's town to Kapilavastu. He was not interested in the Tilaurâ-Koṭ town, and, therefore, passed it by.

Hiuen Tsiang, on the contrary, went first to his Kapilavastu, from which Krakuchandra's town lay nine miles to the south. If Hiuen Tsiang actually visited the towns of the previous Buddhas, he seems to have done so by making an excursion from Kapilavastu. He appears to have gone to the Lumbini garden past the spot which was pointed out to him as the "arrow-well," 30 *li* south-east of the city. I cannot attempt to identify either his "arrow-well," or that of Fa-hien. Both pilgrims are agreed that Râmagrâma was 200 *li* east of the Lumbini garden, and that site will be easily found as soon as somebody can manage to go and look for it.

Map.

The map (Plate II) which I have prepared exhibits in an easily intelligible form my interpretation of the pilgrims' records. I now proceed to justify my identifications in more detail.

Large area of Hiuen Tsiang's Kapilavastu.

The identification of the city on the Bânganga with the Kapilavastu of Hiuen Tsiang may, I think, be accepted as absolutely certain. Some enquirers seem to have overlooked the fact which is obvious on the face of the pilgrim's narrative that the Kapilavastu visited and described by Hiuen Tsiang covered a very large area. The central citadel ("royal precincts" of Beal, "palais" of Julien) alone had a circuit of about two and a half miles according to the pilgrim's estimate, and the ruined monasteries were so numerous that they are described as numbering a thousand or more. These details necessarily imply that the area of the ruins was very extensive. Proposals to identify any individual small section of the ruins, such as Tilaurâ-Koṭ, or Araurâ-Koṭ, with Kapilavastu as a whole exhibit a misunderstanding of the premises.

Object of this investigation.

Before proceeding further with the discussion, I desire the reader to be goo enough to understand that my enquiries to ascertain the position of Kapilavastu are directed solely to the ascertainment of the site or sites visited by the two Chinese pilgrims. I do not profess at present to consider the question of the authenticity of the sites pointed out to the pious pilgrims by the local monkish guides. Whenever that question is considered the enquirer should remember that an interval of at least nine hundred years intervened between the death of Gautama Buddha and the visit of Fa-hien. The more detailed account of Hiuen Tsiang dates from a period about two hundred and thirty years later.

The city on Bângangâ agrees with Hiuen Tsiang's description.

The group of ruins near the Bângangâ agrees well with the description of Hiuen Tsiang. The area bounded by Lori-kî-kudâu, Gutivâ, Tilaurâ-Koṭ, Sâgarwâ, Niglivâ, and Araurâ-Koṭ is amply sufficient to provide room for all the objects described by Hiuen Tsiang as existing in his time, and the remains are sufficiently numerous. Tilaurâ-Koṭ occupies the centre of the position, and is clearly the citadel of the ruined city. In the whole country-side there is no other walled enclosure corresponding to the citadel described by Hiuen Tsiang, of which the walls were still in his time high and massive (*hautes et solides*). In the Tarai no large town has ever existed for the last fifteen hundred years or more, and the demolition of old structures for building material has been very limited in extent. Bricks, if untouched by man, are practically indestructible. Consequently, the citadel seen by Hiuen Tsiang thirteen centuries ago must still be traceable. Tilaurâ-Koṭ, which lies about fifteen miles from the Lumbini garden in a westerly direction, is in the required position. The "arrow-well" which the monks pointed out to the pilgrims at a distance of 30 *li*, or five and a half miles, south-east of the city has not been identified. The site was marked only by a small *stupa* and is not likely to be traceable.

Taulîśvara and Gutivâ.

The Taulîśvara temple at Taulivâ is very probably, as suggested by Mr. Mukherji, the temple of Iśvara mentioned in the Buddhist legends as standing to the east of the city. Thirteen hundred years ago Hiuen Tsiang was unable to ascertain the exact limits of the city, and an explorer now cannot expect to be more fortunate. For topographical purposes I assume the ruins of Lori-kudâu to be the southern boundary of the city. No mention is made of any remains further south. My personal knowledge does not extend further south than Tilaurâ-Koṭ. Remains exist between Tilaurâ and Taulivâ. I am inclined to suppose that Gutivâ, where there is an Asoka pillar, lay outside the southern boundary of the city, and that it may mark the banyan grove which lay half a mile to the south.

Tilaurâ-Koṭ.

The Koṭ of Tilaurâ is by measurement only about a mile in circuit, whereas Hiuen Tsiang estimated the circuit of the "royal precincts" to be about 2 miles. He may have been mistaken, as I was, for I estimated the circuit to be about two miles. Moreover, a triangular patch of ruins exists to the north outside the walls which is not included in Mr. Mukherji's measurements and would add considerably to the circuit if included. Considering the fact that there is no other place in the whole region which can possibly be identified with the "royal precincts" described by Hiuen Tsiang, the identification of them with Tilaurâ-Koṭ can hardly be doubted.

Araurâ-Koṭ and Niglivâ.

Araurâ-Koṭ may or may not have been inside the city boundary.

Niglivâ, with its numerous ancient tanks, doubtless formed part of the city.

Sâgarwâ.

The remains at Sâgarwâ may have been included, but I think it more probable that they represent the supposed scene of the slaughter of the Sâkyas, a short distance north-west of the capital. The fact that in the seventeen small *stupas* opened by Dr. Führer the bricks over the relic or ashes caskets bore representations of weapons indicates that the persons whose cremation is commemorated fell in battle.

Further identification not justified by evidence.

I cannot attempt any further detailed identifications of monuments mentioned by Hiuen Tsiang. The evidence in its present state does not justify such an attempt, and merely plausible guessing adds nothing to knowledge.

Paltâ Devî = town of Krakuchandra.

The town of Krakuchandra was according to Hiuen Tsiang about 50 *li*, some nine or ten miles, in a southerly direction from Kapilavastu. When measurement is made from Lori-kî-kudân, a site apparently suitable is found at Paltâ Devî, situated in a bend of the Jâmuâr river, about three miles on the British side of the frontier. The ancient side includes Musarawâ close to Mr. George Peppé's house. The shrine of Paltâ Devî (Palatâ Devî of Buchanan-Hamilton, "Eastern India," Volume II, page 399,) is of much local celebrity. The existing buildings are small and modern, but they stand on the ruins of a considerable ancient edifice. A broken pillar, worshipped as a Mahâdeo, is said to extend deep down into the ground, and Mr. William Peppé believes it to be an Aśoka pillar. The supposed events in the history of Krakuchandra Buddha were according to Hiuen Tsiang commemorated by three *stupas*, and by an inscribed lion-pillar of Asoka, 30 feet high. The Paltâ Devî site has not been carefully examined, and I can not say how far the existing remains agree with the meagre indications given by the pilgrims. If the broken pillar is really an Asoka pillar, my identification, which is primarily based on the distance from the south end of Hiuen Tsiang's Kapilavastu, receives strong support. I do not know of any other site at the required distance to the south of the capital. Fa-hien's itinerary also justifies the identification of Paltâ Devî with the town of Krakuchandra.

Sisaniâ Pânre=town of Koṇagamanâ.

Both pilgrims agree that Koṇagamanâ's town was five or six miles from Krakuchandra's town. Fa-hien gives the direction as north, Hiuen Tsiang, writing, as usual, with more precision, gives it as north-east, which may be taken as correct. Sisaniâ Pânre (*Report*, page 33) corresponds accurately in distance and direction. The distance from Paltâ Devî is about 5½ miles, and the direction is north-east. The remains seem to be those of an ancient town (*grande ville antique*).

A possible alternative.

It is also possible that the town of Krakuchandra lay a little west of south from the city, and that it should be looked for south of Chândâpâr in the place indicated by a cross on my map, at a distance of about 11 miles from Lori-kî-kudân. In that case Paltâ Devî would represent the town of Koṇagamanâ. I am convinced that the Paltâ Devî site marks the position of either one or the other of the towns of the previous Buddhas. If there are remains in the required position near Chândâpâr, this alternative proposition would be preferable, in as much as it would dispense with the awkward angle involved by diverting Fa-hien's route to Sisaniâ,

What Fa-hien saw at Kapilavastu.

When Fa-hien, about A.D. 406, came to Kapilavastu, the place was a desolate wilderness, with neither king nor people.[1] The only inhabitants were a few monks and a score or two families of the common people. His guides showed him the following twelve sacred spots:—

(1) They exhibited images or representations (? pictures) of the prince (Gautama) and his mother at the time of his conception on the spot where the ancient palace of king Suddhodhana stood(" where formerly was the palace, " *Legge*).

(2 and 3) They showed him *stupas* at the place where the conception was supposed to have taken place, and where the prince turned his chariot after seeing the sick man at the gate:—and they pointed out the localities where,

(4) Asita inspected the marks on the infant;

(5) Gautama tossed the elephant;

(6) The arrow made a spring of water gush out, 30 *li* to the south-east;

(7) Gautama met his father;

(8) Five hundred Sâkyas did reverence to Upâli;

(9) Buddha preached to (" prayed for, " *Giles*) all the Devas, and his father was excluded from the hall;

(10) Buddha sat under a banyan tree, and received the *Sanghâli* robe from his aunt Prajâpati;

(11) King Vaidûrya slew the Sâkyas, at which place a still existing *stupa* was erected; and the guides also pointed out

(12) The field where the prince watched men ploughing.

This last spot was several *li* to the north-east of the city. Professor Legge notes that Fa-hien does not say, as the other translators make him say, that *stupas* were erected to mark the localities numbered (4) to (10). He clearly mentions no more than three *stupas*, and there is not a word about massive citadel walls, or *vihâras*, or Brahmanical temples. Even if a dozen *stupas* were shown to the pilgrim, there would not, I think, be any difficulty in locating so many among the ruins near Piprâvâ. The only allusion to the palace mentions it as a building that had formerly existed, and it is possible that in reality no palace ever existed on the Piprâvâ site.

Hiuen Tsiang's account compared.

Fa-hien simply notes that " there is a royal field, where the heir-apparent sat under a tree and watched men ploughing." (*Giles.*) No indication is given that the spot was marked by any monument, and the distance from the city is given as " several *li*." Hiuen Tsiang puts the spot shown to him as that from which the prince watched the ploughing at a distance of 40 *li*, or 7½ miles, from the city. The " several *li* " of Fa-hien could hardly exceed one mile, or, at the outside, two miles.

---

[1] For quotations from Fa-hien I have consulted and compared all the four versions, namely, (1) Laidlay's, from the French of Rémusat, valuable for the notes; (2) Beal's revised version in " Buddhist Records of the Western World "; (3) Legge's, from a Corean text; and (4) Giles'. The last named aims at being an exact grammatical rendering, and is of value. Professor Legge's version is the latest, and, so far as a reader ignorant of Chinese can judge, seems, to be on the whole, the best. The notes are, however, not very helpful.

For Hiuen Tsiang I have used the versions of Julien and Beal. The French scholar's renderings often seem to be the better. I follow Mr. Beal's spelling of the name of the later pilgrim because it is most familiar to English readers. Mr. Watters writes " Fa-hien " and " Yuan-chuang." By the death of Mr. Watters in January, 1901, Chinese scholarship has lost one of its most brilliant ornaments.

Fa-hien saw only one *stupa* at the place of the massacre of the Sâkyas, whereas Hiuen Tsiang understood that hundreds and thousands of *stupas* marked the locality. The incident numbered (9) in Fa-hien's list is not mentioned by Hiuen Tsiang. The 500 Sâkyas who did reverence to Upâli seem to correspond to the 500 Sâkyas, who, according to Hiuen Tsiang, were converted by preaching. The later pilgrim says that the spot in the banyan grove south of the city where the Buddha met his father was marked by a *stupa* of Asoka. Both pilgrims agree that the spring which gushed forth when the arrow fell was 30 *li* south-east of the capital, and the spot shown to Hiuen Tsiang was marked by a small *stupa*. The agreement only shows that the legend was told to both visitors in the same form. It is quite possible that the actual spots shown to the two were different. The necessary inference from the distances given by Fa-hien is that *his* "arrow-well" was about 8 or 9 miles from the Lumbini garden. Hiuen Tsiang expressly states that *his* "arrow-well" was some 15 miles distance from that point. I therefore conclude that the two pilgrims visited distinct spots, each of which was exhibited as the "arrow-well."

The earlier pilgrim simply noticed the spot where Buddha was supposed to have tossed the elephant. The later writer gives many details of the legend, and notes that the spot was marked by a *stupa*, near which was a *vihâra* of the prince, and another *vihâra* with a likeness of Yasodharâ and her child, supposed to mark the site of the queen's bedroom. The foundations of the school-room were also pointed out. Sites of this class are clearly mythical, and might be placed anywhere by pious guides.

Hiuen Tsiang locates to the north of the palace of the conception a *stupa* commemorating Asita's inspection of the wondrous infant.

Fa-hien seems to have seen but one *stupa* at the eastern gate to mark the spot where Gautama turned his chariot after beholding the sick man. Hiuen Tsiang places a *vihâra*, not a *stupa*, outside each of the four gates, "in which there are respectively figures of an old man, diseased man, a dead man, and a Śraman." (*Beal.*) The differences between the two records seem to indicate that the observers were shown different objects.

Fa-hien declares that a *stupa* was erected where Buddha "appeared mounted on a white elephant when he entered his mother's womb" (*Legge*). Hiuen Tsiang says that the spot was marked by a *vihâra*, which contained a representation (? picture) of the scene.

A tree was shown to Fa-hien as marking the spot where Gautama sat and received a *sanghâli* robe from his aunt Prajâpati. Hiuen Tsiang calls the robe a *Kashâya*, and was shown a *stupa* as marking the spot.

Discrepancies in the accounts of the two pilgrims.

The result of this detailed examination is that, although nearly all the holy places shown to Fa-hien were shown also to Hiuen Tsiang, who notes several others in addition, yet the descriptions vary so materially that it is difficult to believe that the two writers are describing the same places. My inference that the Kapilavastu described by Hiuen Tsiang must be distinct from the Kapilavastu described by the earlier pilgrim was founded solely on the irreconcileable discrepancies between the statements of the two pilgrims concerning the relative distances and bearings of Kapilavastu and neighbouring places. The discrepancies in description now adduced seem to me to give strong support to my proposition.

Agreement as to Lumbini garden and Râmagrâma.

The accounts given by the two pilgrims of the Lumbini garden agree so far as they touch one another. Both authors also agree in placing Lan-mo, or Râmagrâma, 200 *li*, or about 37 to 40 miles east of the Lumbini garden. This circumstance adds yet another proof to the evidence already conclusive that Rummin-dei is the site of the famous garden.[1] It also teaches that the pilgrims' figures are not to be lightly tampered with.

Distance from Srâvasti.

It has been proved that the two pilgrims agree substantially in their estimate of the distance of Kapilavastu from Srâvasti. The distance from Srâvasti to Piprâvâ is slightly greater than that to the city round Tilaurâ-Koṭ, but to compensate for this difference Hiuen Tsiang reckons from a spot north of Srâvasti, while Fa-hien reckons from Srâvasti itself, and probably from the southern gate. This difference in starting point is enough to account for several miles. The statement that the two pilgrims substantially agree in their estimates of the distance between Kapilavastu and Srâvasti is, therefore, not invalidated by the discovery that the Kapilavastu of Fa-Hien lies about 9 miles south-east of the Kapilavastu of Hiuen Tsiang.

No explanation for existence of two Kapilavastus.

If I am asked the reason why, in or about A.D. 406, Piprâvâ was regarded as representing Kapilavastu, whereas in A.D. 635 the city on the Bâṅgangâ was regarded as representing the same place, I can only reply that I do not know the reason, and plead that ignorance concerning events which occurred fifteen hundred years ago is excusable. Hiuen Tsiang ascribes to Asoka Raja the erection of the *stupa* in the banyan grove half a mile south of the city where the Sâkya Tathâgata, after attaining enlightenment, met his father. That locality, as already observed, may be represented by Guṭivâ, and certainly was south of Tilaurâ-Koṭ. If Hiuen Tsiang can be supposed to have been mistaken in assigning this monument to Asoka, it is probable that the emperor, like Fa-hien, visited Piprâvâ, and that the change of the holy places took place during the disturbed period between the downfall of the Gupta empire and the rise of Harshavardhana, that is to say, during the sixth century.[2]

The Asoka pillars.

Asoka is also credited with the erection of *stupas* and pillars at the towns of Krakuchandra and Koṇagamanâ. The two pilgrims evidently visited the same two places as representing these towns. The Asoka pillar of Krakuchandra's town is probably that which is now worshipped as a Mahâdeo at Paltâ Devî. The Koṇagamanâ pillar is doubtless that now lying at the Nigâlî Sâgar. It was probably removed from Sisaniâ, a distance of eight miles, or, if Paltâ Devî be the site of Koṇagamanâ's town, from Pâlta Devî, a distance of about 13 miles. One of the Buddhist

[1] Beal ("Records," II, 25) translates :—"From this going east 300 li or so, across a wild and deserted jungle, we arrive at the kingdom of Lan-mo (Râmagrâma)." Julien (I, 325) translates :—"En partant de ce royaume, il se dirigea vers l'est, et, après avoir fait environ deux cents li à travers des plaines désertes et des forêts sauvages, il arrive au royaume de Lan-mo. (Râmagrâma.)" At the rate of 40 *li* to the *yojana*, this estimate exactly agrees with Fa-hien's statement (Chapter XXIII) that "east from Buddha's birth place, and at a distance of five *yojanas*, there is a kingdom called Râma." Julien is clearly right.

[2] When revising the proofs of this paper in March and June, 1901, I have carefully reconsidered the theory propounded in the text, and have found no reason to change my opinion.

Pâla kings of the eleventh or twelfth century may well have been responsible for the transfer. Buddhist inscriptions of late date have been found at Saheṭ-Maheṭ[1] in the Gonḍâ District to the west and at Kasiâ in Gorakhpur to the east.[2] Mr. Mukherji notes that he formed the opinion that the Nigâlî Sâgar embankments had been repaired. The pillar was probably moved at the time of the repairs, which must have been subsequent to the visit of Hiuen Tsiang, who found the monument in its original position. Of course, Hiuen Tsiang's statement that the Asoka pillars bore inscriptions relating the circumstances of the Nirvâṇa of Krakuchandra Buddha and Koṇagamanâ Buddha simply means that at the time of the pilgrim's visit the Maurya characters had become obsolete and were unintelligible either to him or his guides. The guides, then, after the manner of their kind, invented versions of the inscriptions which they could not read.

Considering that Firoz Shâh conveyed the Asoka pillars at Delhi, one from Mîrath (Meerut), and the other from Topra near Ambâla (Umballa), no difficulty need be felt about the transport of the Koṇagamanâ pillar eight or thirteen miles. Coolies are cheap, and with enough coolies anything can be moved.[3]

The relics of Buddha at Piprâvâ.

According to the well-known legends, which may have some basis of fact, the relics of Gautama Buddha were, immediately after his cremation, divided into eight shares, of which the Sâkyas of Kapilavastu obtained one. Mr. Peppé's *stupa* at Piprâvâ may well be the building erected over the relics of Gautama obtained at his cremation. It is unlikely that the inscription is later than B.C. 400, and it is quite possible that it may be earlier. It is very odd, as Mr. Watters has observed, that neither of the Chinese pilgrims makes the least allusion to the *stupa* erected by the Sâkyas of Kapilavastu over the cremation relics of Gautama. Even Fa-hien, who was taught to regard Piprâvâ as Kapilavastu, was not shown this important monument. I cannot offer any plausible explanation of the omission, which is the more strange, because Fa-hien in his account of Kusinagara alludes to the legend of the division of the relics. (See Postscript.)

The scepticism of Mr. Watters.

The essay of Mr. Watters entitled "Kapilavastu in the Buddhist Books" is well worthy of attention.[4] It is based on the study of original Chinese authorities, and shows clearly that the knowledge of Kapilavastu possessed by Buddhist writers was hazy in the extreme. Mr. Watters writes in a very sceptical spirit, and apparently feels doubts as to the reality of the Sâkya principality in the Tarai. The Piprâvâ inscription, which was not known when Mr. Watters wrote, certainly fixes the Sâkyas in the Tarai, and so limits the range of scepticism.

Ruins near Piprâvâ.

It will be useful to place on record a note of the places in the neighbourhood of Piprâvâ where ancient remains are known to exist. The *stupa* of Buddha's relics near the

---

[1] The Saheṭ-Maheṭ inscription is correctly dated 1176 V. S.=A.D. 1119, as stated by Dr. Hoey. Kielhorn in *Ind. Ant.*, Vol. XXIV, 176, candidly admits that Dr. Hoey's version is an improvement on his own.

[2] This inscription was found near the Mâtâ Kuñwar mediæval image of a Buddha or Bodhisattva near Kasiâ. It does not seem to be dated, but the long text has not yet been edited. Before I quitted India in March, 1900, I sent the stone to the Lucknow Provincial Museum.

[3] Concerning the movements of heavy statues see *J. R. A. S.*, for January 1900, pages 24 and 143.

[4] *J. R. A. S.*, July, 1898, page 533.

village of Piprâvâ stands to the west of the high road from Naugarh, and about half a mile from the frontier. A group of mounds, including apparently *stupas*, lies about half a mile to the west of the relic *stupa*, and there is another mound of ruins more than a quarter of a mile to the east. There are two mounds beyond, that is to the east of, the Sisvâ reservoir and a few miles distant to the south-east in the Dulhâ Grant there are several mounds. A large mass of ruins exists at Piprî, about nine miles from Piprâvâ, three miles south from Birdpur, and about half a mile east from the high road. The remains of what must have been a considerable town exist round the Trigonometrical Survey station at Ghaus, two and a quarter miles from Birdpur. These ruins lie chiefly on the west side of the road, but extend across it, and are separated from the Pipri ruins by not more than a mile. An ancient tank exists at Râmpur, 2½ miles south-west of Piprâvâ.

At a greater distance, may be mentioned remains near Chandâpâr some four miles west from Paltâ Devî; Rummin-dei No. 2 (*Report,* page 4); Katahlâ near this Rummin-dei, a very extensive site described by Buchanan-Hamilton ("Eastern India", II, 396), and Sirwant, about 3½ miles south of Chillia police station. In an easterly direction I suspect that many ruins may exist, but at Pillar No. 40 the boundary bends southward and Nepalese territory projects in the British dominions, so that details are not known.

Remains north of Gorakhpur District.

There is no doubt that many remains of interest exist along the northern boundary of the Gorakhpur District, some in British, and some in Nepalese territory. But this part of the country is very difficult of access and is unhealthy, so that it is rarely visited by Europeans. As Mr. Mukherji notes (page 59), an Asoka pillar is reported to exist north of the Nichlaul police station, in about 27° 28′ N. lat. and 83° 49′ E. long.

The Rohini river, which falls into the Râptî near Gorakhpur, is mentioned in some of the Buddhist legends as flowing between Kapilavastu and the other Sâkya city, variously named Koli, Devadâha, or Vyâghra-pura. The map shows the western branch of this river about fourteen miles east of the Tilâr, and the eastern branch, also called the Baghela, three miles further on. Dr. Hoey, who visited this part of the frontier early in 1898, reports that the *tappa*, or subdivision, east of the Baghela is known as Baghaur, and with great probability connects these names with Vyâghra-pura. On the bank of the river Jharahi, about two miles south-east from Parâsî-Bazaar, which is five or six miles north of the frontier, Dr. Hoey found a well-preserved *stupa,* and in a river-bed some four miles north of Parâsî, he found the capital of a pillar, "3½ or 4 feet in diameter, and well carved" (*Pioneer,* 25th March, 1898).

Probable site of Koli.

I think that the town of Koli (Devadâha, or Vyâghra-pura) may be located on the Baghela river, some seventeen or eighteen miles east of Rummin-dei.

The Sâkya country.

I am disposed to think that the Sâkya country was the Terai extending eastward from the point where the Râptî leaves the hills to the Little Gandak, that is to say, that it lay between the kingdoms of Srâvasti and Râmagrâma. (E. long. 81° 53′ to 83° 49′.) The southern boundary cannot at present be defined.

Râmagrâma.

The distance eastward from the Lumbini garden to Râmagrâma kingdom was nearly 40 miles. The capital will, I think, be found in Nepâlese territory near the frontier, north, or a little east of north from Nichlaul police station. A village named Dharmauli (= Dharmapuri) is on the frontier, and the name has a Buddhist look.

The "ashes *stupa*."

The "ashes *stupa*", where the ashes of Gautama Buddha's funeral pyre were supposed to be enshrined, is probably the great *stupa* at Lauṛiyâ Navandgaṛh in the Champâran District. Mr. Mukherji informs me that the name Navandgaṛh given by Cunningham is incorrect, and that Nandangaṛh should be substituted.

Kusinagara.

Kusinagara must, in my opinion, be far in the interior of Nepâl, and certainly across the first range of hills.[1]

Programme of exploration.

The programme of exploration recommended by Mr. Mukherji is probably beyond the powers of the Archæological Survey as at present organized, and would in any case require several seasons for its execution. An obvious difficulty is that most of the sites are within Nepâlese territory, and however great may be the good will of the Nepâlese central government, exploration in foreign territory is much more troublesome than in a British District.

Srâvasti.

The site which I believe to be that of Srâvasti is in such a remote situation and so buried in forest that it is not likely to be ever minutely surveyed. If the Nepâlese authorities consent, a fortnight might be profitably spent in superficial research. Attention should be specially directed to the verification or reputation of the reports current about the existence of Asoka pillars. Kusinagara, at the other end of the Buddhist holy land, may lie buried in a place for ever inaccessible to European research.

Kusinagara.

Kapilavastu of Hiuen Tsiang.

At the site of Hiuen Tsiang's Kapilavastu there is ample scope for prolonged research, which should be so conducted as to avoid unnecessary destruction. The mounds at Guṭivâ and Lori-kudân, and the interior of Tilaurâ-Koṭ seem specially deserving of attention.

Paltâ Devî and Chândâpûr.

Paltâ Devî should be surveyed, and the country about Chândâpûr should be examined in order to determine the site of Krakuchandra's town. These localities are in the Bastî District, in British territory.

Sisaniâ Pânre.

Sisaniâ Pânre does not look promising for excavation, but the locality should be surveyed.

Piprâvâ.

The Piprâvâ group of ruins is of exceptional interest. The *stupa* containing relics of Buddha opened by Mr. Peppé is certainly one of the oldest buildings in India, and it is very desirable that this building should be thoroughly cleared, and the procession paths and all other structural details fully surveyed. Much excavation remains to be

[1] I shall shortly publish an essay on the position of Kusinagara and the "ashes *stupa*."

done before the plan and arrangement of the neighbouring edifices can be understood. I know that the Messrs. Peppé are ready and anxious to promote further investigations and I have no doubt that the other sharers in the estate, if properly approached, will give their consent. It is quite possible that other early inscriptions may be found in some of the buildings.

Rummin-dei.

The Rummin-dei mound, which unquestionably represents the Lumbini garden, the traditional birth place of Gautama Buddha, is worthy of detailed survey and thorough exploration. The mound is a compact manageable mass of ruins, and seems to include all the eight *stupas* mentioned by Hiuen Tsiang, as well as the fine temple partially exposed by Mr. Mukherji. A month's work with an adequate supply of labour would probably be required on this site. Provisions are procurable without much difficulty.

Northern boundary of Gorakhpur.

It is desirable that a preliminary reconnaissance survey should be run along the northern boundary of the Gorakhpur District, on both sides of the frontier, and the position of the principal ancient sites ascertained. Such a survey will probably result in the certain determination of the sites of both Koli and Râmagrâma, and some Asoka pillars may possibly be discovered. The working season in this region is very limited. Before Christmas the climate is too feverish to allow of exploration with safety. January and February are the best months for work. It is, perhaps, just possible that Râmagrâma may lie to the east of the Gandak at Bâwan Gaṛhi near Sohariâ in the Râmnagar pargana of the Champâran District, but the distance from Rummin-deî to Bâwan Gaṛhi is too great, and I think it more probable that Râmagrâma will be found about north-north-east from Nichlaul in Nepalese territory, near Dharmauli.

Champâran District.

The Champâran District presents an immense field for research. The most important sites are at Lauṛiyâ-Nandangaṛh (Navandgaṛh), which I think represents the "ashes *stupa*,"[1] and at Basâṛ or Basâṛh, the ancient Vaisâli. Dr. Hoey has recently expressed doubts as to the identity of Basâṛh and Vaisâli,[2] but the identification can be fully proved. Cunningham's account of the place is extremely defective and unsatisfactory.[3]

The remarkable mound at Chânkîgaṛh, which is probably a fortress, should be surveyed,[4] and the remains at Râmpurwâ, where two Asoka pillars exist, also require survey.[5] I think that the road from Pâṭaliputra (Patna) to Kuśinagara passed through Basâṛh (Vaisâli), Kesariya,[6] Lauṛiyâ-*Ararâj*,[7] Bettiah, Lauṛiyâ-Nandangaṛh, Chânkîgaṛh, Râmpurwâ, and the Bhiknâ Thori pass. It probably then went round by a circuitous route along the existing road through the Churiâ Ghâtî pass. Ruins are said to exist at Bângaṛh and other places across the Bhiknâ Thori pass. The country beyond the passes is closed to Europeans.

---

[1] Cunningham, *Arch. Rep.* I, 68—74, XVI, 104; XXII, 42.
[2] *J. A. S. B.*, Part I, Vol. LXIX (1900), p. 78.
[3] *Arch. Rep.* I, 55—64; XVI, 6—16, 34, 89—91. The name is बसाड़ or बसाढ़.
[4] "Chankee" of the maps; called "Chandki" by Mr. Garrick in *Arch. Rep.*, XVI, 109; and miscalled "Jânkî Kot" or "Garh" by Mr. Carlleyle, in *ibid* XXII, 50. Mr. Mukherji visited this place and gave me some notes about it.
[5] *Arch. Rep.* XVI, 110; XXII, 51.
[6] *Arch. Rep.* I, 64—67; XVI, 16.
[7] *Arch. Rep.* I, 67. The Asoka inscriptions have been edited by Bühler in *Epigraphia Indica*.

This list of sites for exploration might be indefinitely extended. Enough has been said to show how unfounded is the notion which was current a few years ago, that all needful archæological exploration had already been done. In reality, with very few exceptions, the work accomplished is of the nature of a very imperfect reconnaissance survey, and nearly everything in the way of detailed, accurate, study of the innumerable remains in Northern India remains to be done. The work still left undone is sufficient to occupy generations of explorers.

Imperfection of survey to date.

VINCENT A. SMITH.

CHELTENHAM;
November 1900.

POSTSCRIPT.

Professor Rhys Davids has favoured me with a proof of his paper entitled "Asoka and the Buddha-relics" which will appear in the July number of the Journal of the Royal Asiatic Society, and from which I extract the following passage:—

"Our oldest authority, the Mahā-parinibbāna Suttanta, which can be dated approximately in the fifth century B.C.,[1] states that after the cremation of the Buddha's body at Kusinārā, the fragments that remained were divided into eight portions. These eight portions were allotted as follows:—

1. To Ajātasattu, king of Magadha.
2. To the Licchavis of Vesālī.
3. To the Sâkyas of Kapilavastu.
4. To the Bulis of Allakappa.
5. To the Kolias of Rāmagāma.
6. To the brahmin of Veṭhadīpa.
7. To the Mallas of Pâvā.
8. To the Mallas of Kusinārā.

Droṇa, the brahmin who made the division, received the vessel in which the body had been cremated. And the Moriyas of Pipphalivana, whose embassy claiming a share of the relics only arrived after the division had been made, received the ashes of the funeral pyre.

Of the above, all except the Sâkyas and the two brahmins based their claim to a share on the fact that they also, like the deceased teacher, were Kshatriyas. The brahmin of Veṭhadīpa claimed his because he was a brahmin; and the Sâkyas claimed theirs on the ground of their relationship. All ten promised to put up a cairn over their portion, and to establish a festival in its honour.

Of these ten cairns, or *stupas* only one has been discovered—that of the Sâkyas. The careful excavation of Mr. Peppé makes it certain that this *stûpa* had never been opened until he opened it. The inscription on the casket states that "This deposit of the remains of the Exalted One is that of the Sâkyas, the brethren of the Illustrious One." It behoves those who would maintain that it is not, to advance some explanation of the facts showing how they are consistent with any other theory. We are bound in these matters to accept, as a working hypothesis, the most reasonable of various possibilities. The hypothesis of forgery is in this case simply unthinkable. And we are fairly entitled to ask: "If this *stupa* and these remains are not what they purport to be, then what are they?" As it stands the inscription, short as it is, is worded in just the manner most consistent with the details given in the Suttanta. And it advances the very same claim (to relationship) which the Sâkyas alone are

---

[1] That is substantially, as to not only ideas, but words. There was dotting of *i*'s and crossing of *t*'s afterwards. It was naturally when they came to write these documents that the regulation of orthography and dialect arose. At the time when the Suttanta was first put together out of older material, it was arranged for recitation, not for reading, and writing was used only for notes. See the introduction to my "Dialogues of the Buddha," vol. i.

stated in Suttanta to have advanced. It does not throw much light on the question to attribute these coincidences to mere chance, and so far no one has ventured to put forward any explanation except the simple one that the *stupa* is the Sâkya tope."

My identification of the Piprâvâ site with the Kapilavastu of Fa-hien rests upon the pilgrim's description of his itinerary. Professor Rhys Davids by a wholly independent line of argument arrives at the same conclusion that Kapilavastu is represented by the Piprâvâ group of ruins. I am convinced that Professor Rhys Davids' argument is sound and that the *stupa* opened by Mr. Peppé really contained the relics of the Sâkya sage enshrined by his Sâkya brethern shortly after his decease and cremation.

If the correctness be admitted of the conclusion which Professor Rhys Davids and I have reached by wholly independent processes of reasoning, it is plain that the Piprâvâ group of ruins is for many reasons of the highest importance, and that the systematic survey and exploration of the locality by a competent expert would be a matter of world-wide interest.

But I cannot discern any prospect of the work being done.

V. A. S.

3rd June 1901.

CONTENTS.

CHAPTER I.

CHAPTER II.

CHAPTER III.

CHAPTER IV.

CHAPTER V—*continued.*

CHAPTER V.

CHAPTER VI.

CHAPTER VII.

LIST OF PLATES.

XVIII. Rummin-dei—Figure 1. General plan of the ruins and mounds.
Do. 2. Sketch section of do. do. east to west.
Do. 3. Sketch section of the ruin, etc., and mounds north to south.
Do. 4. Section on A. B. of Mâyâdevi's Temple.

XIX. Rummin-dei—*Photographs*—
Figure 1. View of the ruins from the west.
Do. 2. View of the ruins from the south.

XX. Rummin-dei—Figure 1. Plan of Mâyâdevi's Temple, so far as exhumed.
Do. 2. Plan of the pillar enclosure.
Do. 3. Section of do. do.
Do. 4. Detail of the Priyadarsi inscription.

XXI. Rummin-dei—Detail plan and elevation of the plinth north façade, western half.

XXII. Rummin-dei—*Photographs*—
Figure 1. Mâyâdevi Temple, showing four periods of buildings.
Do. 2. Ornamented plinth of the Temple, north-west corner.

XXIII. Rummin-dei—*Photographs*—
Figure 1. Small Stupa south-west of Mâyâdevi Temple.
Do. 2. Do. do. south of do. do.

XXIV. Rummin-dei—Figure 1. Statue of Târâdevi of Varahi defaced.

XXIV*a*. „ Do. 2. Group statue of Mâyâdevi.

XXV. Sainâ-Mainâ—Figure 1. Two pedestals of temple statues, plan and section.
Do. 2. Pilaster with Tibetan and other inscriptions.
Do. 3. Amalakas that crowned temple-*sikharas* with one section.
Do. 4. Six relics of old sculpture.
Do. 5. Sketch map.

XXVI. Dohni, etc.—Figure 1. Two pedestals of pillars at Rummin-dei.
Do. 2. Six relics of sculpture at do.
Do. 3. Durga at Bari Sisâniâ.
Do. 4. Sculptured door at Dohni, partly restored.

XXVII. Piprâvâ—Figure 1. General plan of stupa, Sanghârâma, Vihâra, etc., north of the village of.
Do. 2. Section of Stupa.
Do. 3. Stone box from Stupa.
Do. 4. General plan of the ruins, south-west of the village.

XXVIII. Piprâvâ—*Photographs*—
Figure 1. View of the Stupa, so far as exhumed from south.
Do. 2. Five relic caskets from the stone box Figure No. 3 of the above plate.

All these plates were prepared by me in 1899, except plates XI, XII, figure 5 of XV and photographs in plate X and figure 2 of XXVIII, which were done in 1898, under Dr. Führer's supervision. But I have added the key-plans in plates XI and XII.

P. C. MUKHERJI,
Archæologist.

24th August 1899.

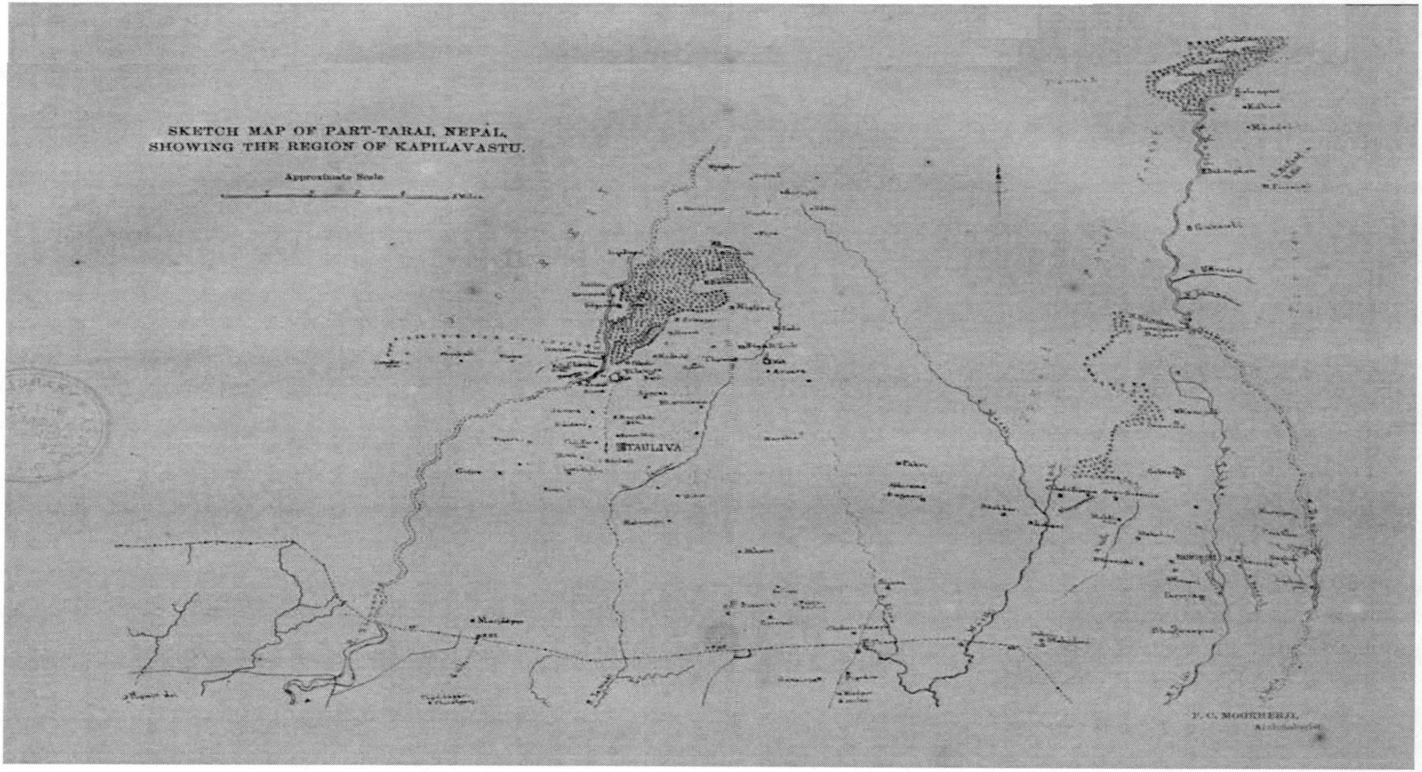
SKETCH MAP OF PART-TARAI, NEPÂL,
SHOWING THE REGION OF KAPILAVASTU.
Approximate Scale
TAULIVA
P. C. MOOKHERJI,

CHAPTER I.

INTRODUCTION.

I. TOPOGRAPHY OF THE TARAI, NEPÂL. (Plate I).

SINCE there is no map of the Tarai, it is not easy to examine the region of the ancient and now forgotten Sâkya-kingdom. There is no road in any direction, the pedestrians travelling in the fields and across *nullahs* and streams, which are seldom bridged. The cart track is so circuitous, that it takes at least double the direct distance before the bullock carts reach their destination.

No Map of Tarai exists.

The Tarai is a flat country, crossed by mountain streams, which flow from north to south, and at short distances from one another. Of these streams, Bânganga and Dâno or Kuṛhâ are the largest; while Jâmuâr, Siswâ, Mârthi, Kothi, and Tilâr, which are between the two largest, are of smaller breadth. The Tarai (literally *Talâi* from Sanskrit *Tala*—below or lower region) is generally cultivated, excepting those parts, which are covered with forests. One forest extends westward from the Bângangâ and northward from Chitrâ-dei. A smaller one is from Tilaurâ on south, to Niglivâ on east, Bikuli on the north-east, and Jagdîspur and Sâgarwâ on the west. Two more forests I saw on my way to Sainâ Mainâ, one extending westward from near Sûrajpurâ, the other on my right, about a mile off. The forest of Sainâ Mainâ is along the foot of the hills, extending east and west, how far I have not seen. Since the forests are all reserved by the Nepâl Government, nobody being allowed to cut even for fuel, they are full of wild animals, which generally intrude upon the neighbouring villages; as I saw one tiger almost attacking me one day near the ruins of Tilaurâ-koṭ; so that exploration of the ruins was not altogether without risks and difficulties.

Nature of the country.

The sites of ancient ruins may be divided into two main groups. The western one consists of Sisaniâ, Gutivâ, Lori-Kudân, Taulivâ, Aṛauṛâ-kot, and Bikuli with Chitrâ-dei and Tilaurâ-koṭ in the centre, which I propose to identify with Kapilavastu. The second group is that of Rummin-dei with Sainâ Mainâ on the north, the two Sisaniâs on the west, and Dohni on the south-west. To these two groups may be added a third,—that of Piprâvâ, which occupies the southern apex of the triangle, made up with the other two.

Sites of ruins grouped into three.

But to map out this tract, which was the first duty entrusted to me, required a good deal of travelling in different directions, for which purpose I had insufficient time. I had only one or two marches, while removing my camp;—two from Piprâvâ to Tilaurâ, one from Tilaurâ to Rummin-dei and, after paying a flying visit to Sainâ Mainâ from Rummin-dei, back to Piprâvâ. I had therefore to consult the little compass attached to my watch, or the sun, while journeying,—and thus took the bearings. And counting the distance by the hours of march, and from what I heard from the villagers, I jotted down from memory what I saw when I reached camp. These

Insufficient explorations and how my map was done.

jottings are the basis of the map I have compiled for this Report, which, I think, is reliable, so far as it goes for rough consultation. My map has also been, so far as possible, connected with and based on sheet No. 188, Revenue Map of North-Western Provinces and Oudh, and on scale of one inch to a mile. (See Plate No. 1.)

II. Previous Explorations.

General Cunningham's Map not satisfactory.

I need not dwell upon the identifications of General Cunningham and his assistant, which did not yield satisfactory results. That Kâsiâ was not Kusinagar, was proved by Mr. Vincent A. Smith in his "Remains near Kasia." And that Bhuilâ Tâl did not fulfil the conditions of Kapilavastu, was noted by scholars as soon as the so-called discovery was announced. When I was studying the Lives of the Buddha from the Nepâlese and Tibetan sources, some fifteen years ago, I noted that Kapilavastu was situated near the Himâlaya mountains and in the Madhyadesa; which statement did not support the identification of the Bhuilâ Tâl. Naturally I was led to look for the site in the Nepâlese Tarai, somewhere near where the modern Rohin flows.

Discovery of the Nigâli pillar.

In March 1893, the discovery of a Priyadarsi pillar, by Major Jaskaran Sing of Balrâmpur, at Bairât,—a deserted site in Pargana Kolhwa of Tehsil Nepâlgunj was announced, which news went the round of newspapers in the spring of 1893 and raised great hopes in the antiquarian world. In March 1895, Dr. Führer was deputed to take estampages. He could not find this *Lâṭ*, but instead found another at Niglivâ on the bank of a large tank, called Sâgar. The inscription recorded the pilgrimage of King Priyadarsi, who had, in the 14th year of his reign, increased the Stupa of Kanaka-muni.

Dr. Führer's deputations.

This discovery raised high hopes amongst Orientalists. Next year Dr. Führer was again deputed to advise in the excavation of Konagamanâ's Stupa, which, however, has not been hitherto undertaken; nor has the Stupa even been found. He went from Niglivâ to Rummin-dei, where another Priyadarsi *Lâṭ* had been discovered; and an inscription, about 3 feet below surface, had been opened by the Nepâlese. The inscription recorded the fact of King Priyadarsi's visiting Lumbinigrâmâ, where Buddha was born, in the 21st year of his reign. This fact, with the name of Rummin-dei,—the corruption of Lumbinidevi,—at once set at rest all doubts as to the exact site of the traditional birth-place of Gautama Buddha. The key to the site of Kapilavastu being thus found, Dr. Führer went north-west and very vaguely located the site amidst jungles and the villages of Ahirauli, Siunagar, and Ramâpurâ on the south, and Jagdispur on the north. (*Progress Report* for 1897, page 4.) He also identified Nâbhikâ, the birth-place of Krakuchandra with Lori-Kudân and Gutivâ (page 19, *Sâkya Muni's Birth-Place*).

Discovery of Rummin-dei Pillar with Priyadarsi inscription.

His third tour.

In 1898, Dr. Führer was again deputed to the Tarai to assist the Nepâl Government with advice and suggestions as regards the best course to be followed in the excavation on the sites of Kapilavastu; for which purpose the Darbâr had sanctioned a sum of Rs. 2,000. Finding some ruined mounds in the forest of Sâgarwâ, and near the tank Sâgar, whence the village-name is derived, the Doctor halted here for about two months, superintending the excavations, which had been commenced in the previous year by General Kharga Singh, the Governor of Pâlpâ. Excavations were started on 22nd December 1897, and continued till the beginning of March 1898; about 200 coolies, mostly *Thârus*, being employed for a week at a time, who returned to their villages; and then a fresh relay of labourers took their place. Several Stupas were found and ruthlessly destroyed. The large number of the Stupas, which he identified as the "Massacre of the Sâkyas" were no sooner traced than destroyed in the hope of finding relics, which, however, were very poor, consisting of a few carved bricks, relic-vessels or caskets, containing some gold *Nâgas*, greenish crystals, beads, ruby, and pieces of bones. His alleged discovery of several inscriptions in "pre-Asoka" characters has been proved to be not based on facts. Altogether his results were very unsatisfactory and not less conflicting. His *Monograph* and *Progress Reports* have been found to be full of mistakes.

Discovery of a pre-Asoka inscription and relics at Piprâvâ.

Another important *find* was announced in January of the last year, when Mr. W. Peppé excavated the mound at Piprâvâ, in the core of which, and in the rectangular chamber, he discovered a large stone-box, in which were found five caskets,—four of soapstone and one crystal, containing bones, gold stars, and beads of sorts, as also some figures, etc. But the most important of these finds was an inscription in the "pre-Asoka" characters, recording that this was the relic (*Sariras*) of the Buddha, enshrined by his Sâkya relatives. This inscription, like those of Rummin-dei and Niglivâ, showed that the Kapilavastu region must be very close to them, which surmise subsequent investigations sustained.

Mr. Mukherji's deputation for two months.

After Dr. Führer's retirement, I was deputed by the Government of the North-Western Provinces and Oudh to the Tarai to continue exploration. Major Waddell, I.M.S., also received permission from the Government of India to join in the investigation. That gentleman preferred to work independently; and I am alone responsible for the investigations recorded in this Report. I was assisted by one draftsman, who joined me later on. The results will show how far I have utilized the short time I had at my disposal.

III. Narrative of my Tour.

Tour commenced.

Receiving instructions from Mr. Vincent A. Smith, Commissioner of Fyzabad, and the Hon'ble Mr. C. W. Odling, C.S.I., Secretary and Chief Engineer to Government, North-Western Provinces and Oudh, I left Lucknow on the 23rd January last, and, continually journeying, without making any halt, reached Taulivâ, the head-quarters of the Nepâlese Tarai, on the evening of the 25th. The next morning, I went to Niglivâ and saw Major Waddell. My further proceedings were temporarily arrested by orders from Government, and I returned to Gorakhpur. On the receipt of a fresh telegram from Government, I proceeded again to Nepâl, and began, on 3rd February last, exploration and excavation at the Tilaurâ-koṭ and its neighbourhood, which impressed me as very promising of results. On the 6th, I visited the ruins at Sâgarwâ, which disappointed me as not the site of Kapilavastu, located by Dr. Führer. But closer inspection showed me that Tilaurâ-koṭ was

Exploration and excavation begun at Tilaurâ-koṭ.

most like y the city of the Buddha's father. I went on excavating the local mounds and exploring the neighbourhood till the 9th, when Major Waddell, who was up to this time away, came and suddenly stopped all excavations and, telling me to prepare plans of the ruins at Sâgarwâ and Tilaurâ, went away the same morning.

Major Waddell interrupts my work.

Accordingly, I engaged myself in surveying and drawing till the 20th, when I received a pencil note from Major Waddell, who left Nepâl on the 22nd, informing me that he was again going out, exploring the country, and that I should now continue the excavations. Accordingly, returning from Sâgarwâ, I began again excavations on a very large scale at Tilaurâ-koṭ and Chitrâ-dei, and, completing the exploration for several miles around in order to prepare a rough map, as instructed by Mr. Vincent A. Smith, I marched, on 11th March, towards Rummin-dei, the Lumbini-vana of the Buddhistic geography, which I reached the next day.

Ancient monuments exhumed at Rummin-dei.

After clearing the jungles, I minutely examined the big mound and set the Nepâlese coolies to excavate at the promising places. From the very commencement, the diggings brought out to light several remains, not less successfully than at Tilaurâ and Chitrâ-dei. The principal find was the anterior temple of Mâyâdevi, of which the beautifully ornamented plinth in brick exists. Remains of several small Stupas and other edifices were also exposed.

On the 19th, I visited the ruins of Sainâ Mainâ at the foot of the hills and hidden in the thick forest of sâl. The days became so hot now that the Nepâlese Captain and his men left for the hills; and myself and my draftsman fell sick. Finishing, therefore, my survey, and taking photographs, as quickly I could, I left Rummin-dei on the 29th March, and exploring the ruins of the two Sisaniâs, reached Piprâvâ the same day. Here I took sketches and photographs, excavating here and there. I visited a third Sisaniâ in Nepâlese Tarai and a second Rummin-dei about four miles west of Chândâpâr, and returned to Lucknow on the 5th April last.

Return to Lucknow.

Insufficient time.

The actual time taken by the Nepâl Tour is, therefore, about two months, of which for about six weeks I had unimpeded work. And considering the results, I trust that I may be credited with having made the best use of the insufficient time I had at my disposal.

Disadvantages I laboured under.

In my late tour I was rather badly equipped; for both the Survey and Drawing implements and the photographic apparatus were old and not in good order, which gave me a great deal of trouble in my work. I was allowed only one draftsman, and he joined me late. And my work grew so much in exploration, direction, supervision of excavations and taking notes, that I hardly found time for drawing on the spot. I took several sketches with detailed measurements. And latterly my draftsman and I fell sick. Though labouring under these disadvantages, I succeeded in gathering a mass of information and illustrations and made a lot of discoveries, of which the identification of Kapilavastu might be the most important. The results are embodied in this Report.

Nepâlese establishment and grants.

The establishment on the part of the Nepâl Government, which was attached to my party, consisted of a Captain (Bhimsen Chhatri) and a gang of 12 *Pâhâṛi* diggers, supplemented by men from the plains, as occasion required. Of last year's grant of Rs. 2,000, there was a saving of Rs. 800. This year's sanction for excavation was Rs. 2,000+800=Rs. 2,800 granted by the Durbar, of which only about Rs. 300 were expended. And I understand that there is about Rs. 2,500 still available for next year's work without the necessity of further grant.

Great help from Mr. V. A. Smith.

In conclusion, I cannot sufficiently feel grateful to Mr. Vincent A. Smith, whose scholarly instructions and help enabled me to discharge successfully the duties entrusted to me. I should also thank Babu Shohrat Singh of Chândâpâr, who, at his request, gave me great help.

CHAPTER II.

HISTORY OF KAPILAVASTU.[1]

IN prehistoric times, according to Buddhist legends, when the solar line ruled over the Kosala kingdom in great prosperity, a descendant of Ikshwâku I, known as Birudhaka or Sujâtta lost his first queen, by whom he had four sons and five daughters. He married a second queen, by whom he had a son.[2] She claimed succession to the throne for her son; and the old king was persuaded to yield to her demands. The sons and daughters of the first queen were therefore sent away on exile from Potala or Sâketa,[3] the capital of the Kosala kingdom. The princes with their followers proceeded in a northern direction through large forests, which thickly covered the land. They arrived at an unpeopled wild,[4] where was the hermitage of a saint, Kapila by name; near which flowed a river, mentioned by some authorities as Bhâgirathi,—most probably the Bân-gangâ of the present day. With the permission of the *Rishi*, the royal brothers founded a town here which they named after the saint, *Kapilavastu*, literally the seat of Kapila. And in order to preserve the purity of their race, the four brothers married the four younger sisters, appointing the eldest as queen-mother. Hearing this, their father, the king of Potala, exclaimed "*Sâkya, Sâkya;*" "well done, well done;" whence the well known name of *Sâkya* was derived. It may also have been derived from the Sâka tree,—as the tribe of the Sâla forest. These Sâkyas were of the Kshattriya caste of the clan of *Gautama;* whence the Buddha is sometimes known as Gautama, vulgarised in Burmese as "Gaudama." For the same reason, his step-mother, Prajâpati, is also called Gautamî. From the Sâkyas, his followers, in the lifetime of the Buddha, were known as Sâkya-puttiya Samanas.

Prehistoric period.

Foundation of Kapilavastu.

Derivation of Sâkya and Gautama and Sâkya-puttiya Samanas.

The eldest sister, Priyâ, was, in course of time, struck with white leprosy, which being thought infectious, she was exiled to a cave in a forest near a river. At the same time, it so happened, that the king of Benares, Râma by name, was attacked by the same disease, and had therefore to resign his kingdom to his son, and to retire into the same forest to die. But by a miraculous coincidence, he was cured, while seated under a kolan or kalau tree (*Nauclea cordifolia*), and seeing the queen in the same condition cured and married her. His son, hearing his recovery, came here and, on his refusal to return to Benares, built a town with walls, tanks and every needful defence and

---

[1] Compiled from (1) Bigandet's *Legend of the Gaudama* from the Burmese; (2) S. Hardy's *Manual of Buddhism* from the Ceylonese; (3) Rockhill's *Life of the Buddha* from the Tibetan; (4) R. Mittra's *Lalita Vistâra* from Nepâlese; (5) Alabaster's *Wheel of Law* from the Siamese; (6) Rhys David's *Buddhism* from the Ceylonese; (7) Kern's *Buddhism* from the Ceylonese; (8) Edkin's *Chinese Buddhism*; (9) Aswaghosa's *Buddha-charita* from the Chinese by S. Beal; (10) Watter's *Kapilavastu* in *R. A. S. Journal* for 1898; and (11) *Sacred Books of the East*, Volumes on *Vinaya* and *Sutras*.

[2] These legends have been often printed; but I reproduce them, because they are necessarily referred to in the course of discussion as to the identification of the holy places.

[3] Benares is mentioned by both Bigandet in his *Gaudama*, page 10, and S. Hardy in his *Manual of Buddhism*, page 131.

[4] "There was a great forest of Sâka (Sâla) trees on the bank of a lake and on the lower slopes of the Himalâya." *Ambatharutta* of the *Digha-Nikaya* III, 1—15.

ornament. The town was called Koli or Kaulya from the kalau tree (*Nauclea cordifolia*), in which the king at first took shelter. It was also called Vyâghra-pura from a tiger, by whose means the princess was discovered in the cave. It was also called Devadâha or Devahrada,[5] the tank of the gods; and the descendants of the king were known as *Kolies*, between whom and the Sâkyas a close affinity was established by intermarriages. Between these two towns flowed a small river Rohini (Bigandet's *Gaudama*, page 12). On the banks of the Rohini or Rohita were gardens. The Koli Râjâ appeared to be subordinate to that of Kapilavastu. There were Kolians also at Râmagrâma, where they erected, long after, a Stupa over the one-eighth of the relics of the Buddha they got at Kusinagar. The king of Kapilavastu, who was no better than a great landlord, like the Tâluqdar of our days, appeared to be subordinate to the monarch of Kosala as subsequent events showed.

Foundation of Koli or Devadâha.

From Ulkâmukha, the name of the eldest brother, the first king of Kapilavastu, to Dhanadurga or Jayasena, the great-grandfather of the Buddha, there intervened 82,010 reigns. The contemporary of Jayasena was Aukaka of Devadâha. The former had a son, Singhahanu, and a daughter, Jasodhârâ. The latter had a son Anjana and a daughter Kânchanâ. Kânchanâ was married to Singhahanu, and Jasodharâ to Anjana. This Anjana, the king of Devadâha, is well known in Buddhistic history as correcting an era, then current and known as *kaudza*, in which great error had crept. Correcting the errors with the help of Dewala, a celebrated hermit, he did away with the era 8640, on a Saturday on the new moon of *Tabaong* or *Phalguna* (March) and established his own on Sunday next on the first day of the waxing moon of the month of *Tagos* (*Chaitra*) in 691 B. C., which was afterwards known as the Grand Epoch or the Anjana era. (Bigandet's *Gaudama*, page 13.)

Historical period begins with Jayasena and Singhahanu.

Institution of a new era by Anjana of Devadâha.

In the 10th year of the new era, Suddhodana was born of Kânchanâ, the sister of Anjana, who also had two sons, Suprabuddha and Dandapani, and two daughters, Mâyâ and Prajâpati, Mâyâdevi being born in the 12th year. Suddodhana was taught in the sciences by Kâladewala, the chief counsellor of Singhahanu. Anjana married his two daughters to Suddhodana, while the latter was in his 18th year, and in the 28th of the new era. At Devadâha, the marriage was celebrated in an immense building, especially erected out of the town and in a grove of mango trees, in the middle of which a spacious hall was arranged with infinite art. (Bigandet's *Gaudama*, page 15.) While yet a prince, Suddhodana repulsed the hillmen of the Pândava tribe, who raided in his country.

Suddhodhana.

Shortly after his marriage, his father, Singhahanu, died; and Suddhodana became king, who, with his amiable wife, Mâyâdevi, observed the five precepts and ten royal duties. According to a Chinese version, Mahânâma Vasishtha was his chief minister. His palace at Kapilavastu, called *Dhârtarâshta*, according to *Lalita Vistâra*, had pavilions, doors, gates, windows, rooms, towers, and temples, as also extensive inner apartments, and furnished with musical instruments. The king also improved the town with many

His palace Dhârtarâshtra.

[5] From the separate foundation of this and Kaulya, as given by Bigandet in the Legend of *Gaudama*, pages 12-13, we find that Devadâha was originally a different town from the other.

tanks, roads, squares, crossings, markets, highways, and temples. Jewels appeared pendent under networks over towers, palaces, and gateways; while cloths of various colours were suspended from trees.

The Buddha's life is not so legendary and untrustworthy as generally thought.

Orientalists are in the habit of discrediting the life of the Buddha, because it contains legendary matters. When a story verges on the miraculous, whatever substratum of truth it contains is thrown away as not worth consideration. But we do not throw away wheat, because it contains chaff. What we do is first to separate the wheat from the chaff and utilize it. Now, analysing the Life of the Buddha and taking out the legends, which we can safely relegate to the region of folklore, we find the residue as quite prosaic and common, each event being in its proper place in the natural sequence of cause and effect. All took place in natural order. There is nothing strange, for example, in the fact of a pregnant woman (Mâyâdevi) paying a visit to her father's garden, where she had spent her childhood, and delivering a son suddenly and quite unprepared. This is an ordinary occurrence of human life. But the legend of Brahmâ and other gods helping and protecting her on this occasion is an afterthought and poetical embellishment to heighten belief in the minds of the faithful. The following facts of the Buddha's life are accordingly compiled from the different authorities to show their bearings on the question of the detailed identifications of the sites of Kapilavastu. I have also particularly noted the architectural features of the houses of the time, as recorded in *Lalita Vistâra*.

Siddhârtha's conception.

It was on the 15th of the waxing moon, in the constellation of *Pushya,* month Âshâṛa,[6] when the Sâkyas were celebrating a festival,[7] and Mâyâdevi was observing the fast of the gods, that the future Buddha was conceived. After ten months, Mâyâ expressed a wish to the king to visit her parents at Devadâha. According to another account, her father, Anjana, brought her for the purpose of delivery; as is generally the custom even now in Hindu households. The road between the two towns was made level, strewed with clean sand; plantain trees were planted on each side; and water vessels were placed at regular intervals. The queen was conveyed in a gilt litter to a garden of sâla trees, Lumbini-vana (S. Hardy's *M. B.*, page 144), which was between the two towns, and which her father had constructed for her mother and named after her. A Chinese version says that it was called after the name of the wife of the chief minister Suprabuddha. The inhabitants of both Kapilavastu and Devadâha used to resort here for recreation. Seeing the trees in flower, she alighted here, and being helped by her sister, Prajâpati, she rose and held the branch of a sâl tree, when the pain of delivery suddenly came over her; and a curtain was hurriedly disposed round her. The future Buddha—"the mighty Nârâyana"—was then born, 12 years after Suddhodana's marriage with Mâyâdevi, amidst the rejoicings of all, on Tuesday, full moon, in the month of Vaisâkha, when the Nakshatra was Wisa in the Anjana Era 68, B. C. 623.[8]

His birth in 623 B. C.

Mâyâdevi having died seven days after her confinement, the Bodhisattva with his stepmother was brought back to Kapilavastu with great procession. On the way thereto

[6] Full moon of Assala, early in the morning—S. Hardy's *M. B.*, page 141.

[7] From the 7th to 14th in the month of Assala—S. Hardy's *M. B.*, page 141.

[8] S. Hardy's *M. B.*, page 146. But Bigaudet says on Friday, constellation Withaka, volume 11—p. 71. 15th day of the sixth month of Dog-year, under the astronomical sign Visâkhâ, Alabaster's *Wheel of Law*, or the Siamese Buddha, p. 100; *Lalita-vistara*, p. 157.

was a great temple, where were the images of Siva, Skandha, Nârâyana, Vaisravana, Sakra, Kuvera, Chandra, Surya, Brahmâ, and the Dikpâls.' There he was taken in a chariot, well embellished in the inner apartments, according to the custom of the Sâkyas to seek blessing from the gods. And a few days after a great festival was held to give a name to the young prince. Siddhârtha was the name chosen; and the eight chief astrologers proclaimed that he would become either a *chakravarti* (Universal Monarch) or a *Buddha*. But Kâladevala, otherwise known as Asita, who was the prime minister of his grandfather and had retired to devote the rest of his life to religious meditation, living in a garden near the town or in the mountain Kiskindha or Sarvadhara in the Sâkya country, (*R. A. S. Journal* for 1898, page 550) foresaw that he would certainly attain Buddha-hood.

His name and astrology.

Five months after the birth of Siddhârtha, there was held a festival, when it was the custom of the Sâkyas to cultivate the fields, the king himself leading the way by holding a golden plough. On this occasion, Siddhârtha, though quite a child, sat in meditation under a tree *Jambu* (fig). In his seventh year, a magnificent bath was constructed; and in his 12th (or 16th, Bigandet's *Gaudama*, Volume I, page 51), the king ordered to be built three palaces, called *Ramma, Suramma, and Subha*, suited to the three seasons of the year. They were of the same height, though the first was of nine storeys, the second of seven, and the third of five. (S. Hardy's *M. B.*, page 151.) And on all sides, guards were placed extending to the distance of four miles, that no signs of evil import would catch the sight of the prince. (S. Hardy's *M. B.*, page 151.) *Lalita Vistára*, page 101, describes his palace as handsome, four-sided, four-cornered, with a pavilion on its top, which showed like a thing made by a skilful goldsmith. Within the first pavilion was a jewelled one, which was made of *Ugrasára* sandal wood, within which was a third, where the bedstead was placed.

Ploughing and festival.

Erection of three palaces.

Infant Bodhisattva was sent to the school to learn, under Visvâmitra, writing on a tablet of *Ugrasárá* wood, like the *takhti* of the present day, in excellent ink with a golden pen mounted with jewels. He learnt 64 kinds of alphabets (*Lalita Vistára*, page 182), among which *Bráhmi Kharoshti*, and the letters of Banga, Anga, and Magadha are mentioned. He excelled not only in writing, but in reading of the *Vedas, Negamas, Puránas, Itihâsas*, 18 *Silpas*, and many other sciences; and in exercises and archery, such as shooting the target of an iron boar beyond seven palm trees. Rockhill in his "*Life of the Buddha*" mentions that Siddhârtha learned letters under Kausika, management of elephants under his uncle Sulabha, and archery under Sâkadeva.

His education at school in writing and reading.

It was in the 66th year of his maternal grandfather's era that Siddhârtha was married to Yasodharâ or Gopâ, the daughter of Suprabuddha (or Dandapani according to *Lalita Vistára*, page 201) and Amitâ of Devadâha. And now his palace was described (*Lalita Vistára*, page 226) as furnished with covered terraces, balconies, gateways, windows, halls, and pavilions ornamented with bells, jewels, parasols, flags, pendents, and silken fabrics. His rooms were provided with stairs, decorated with silken carpets, with delightful floors, blue as lapis-lazuli, and with wide and excellent

' Hiuen Tsiang calls this god Iswara; while in some other accounts the image worshipped was that of Yaksha.

corridors, having birds and flowers; also musical instruments, such as conch, trumpet, drum, etc. Before marriage, in 86, Anjana era, he was tested in his Kshatriya accomplishments in a tournament, which was proclaimed by the ringing of bells at Kapilavastu (*Lalita Vistára*, page 203). Gopâ, who was accomplished in writing and composing poetry and well versed in the rules of *Sutras*, planted a flag victory in the arena. In an immense pavilion erected in the court of the palace, Siddhârtha showed his skill, in wielding a bow, which nobody else could hold up, the arrow of which when shot, went, according to a legendary account, some 10 *Krosa* beyond, where it pierced the earth, making a well, since known as Sara-kupa (arrow-well). Bodhisattva, who was compared to Krishna (*Lalita Vistára*, page 191), excelled all the Sâkya youths in the tournament; after which he threw a dead elephant at a deep hollow, known to this day as *Hosti-garta*, two miles beyond the seven walls and moats of the city. (*Lalita Vistára*, page 213.)

Tournament and his excelling all Sâkya youths.

Visvâmitra examined him in reading 12 different parts of sacred writing, caligraphy, painting, and in many kinds of alphabets; while Arjuna, the astrologer, in the calculation of numbers. Siddhârtha also surpassed in running, riding on elephants and horses and driving a chariot, in wrestling, in the use of the goad and lasso, in dice-playing and in the art of decoration and music.

After his marriage, which was celebrated with great éclat, Siddhârtha was appointed *Yuvaráj* (sub-king) and the governor or Chief Magistrate of a neighbouring town, Kâlîshâka (Chinese), where he does not appear to have lived much, for he was confined to his palace-life, because Suddhodana was very much afraid lest he would renounce the secular life and the chance of attaining universal sovereignty. As Siddhârtha grew in years, and rolled in the luxury of a married life, his distaste was distinctly shown, and, flying from palace-life, he used to retire in the evening in a garden, which was his favourite resort, and after bathing in a magnificent tank, to sit on a well-polished stone under a large tree for contemplation. This park is called Lutiloka in a Chinese record from the name of the presiding deity. In order to prevent him, the king built high walls round the palace, excavated a broad moat, hung massive doors, mounted on machines and chains, at the four main gates of the town, where extra guards were stationed. But Bodhisattava having seen the four scenes of an old leper, a dead man, and a monk, while going out of the city for a drive to his garden and thus being impressed with the impermanence of worldly life, effected the great Renouncement, *Mahâbhiniskramana*, in the midnight of Monday, full moon, and constellation Pushya of July in 97, Anjana era, when he was 29 years old (Bigandet, 11-72, says, 96 Anjana era). Leaving his wife and his baby son, Râhula, and descending from his room, he proceeded to the palace of music, lowered the jewelled lattice and getting on a horse by name Kantaka, departed by the East gate, called Mangaladwâra[10] (Lucky gate), beyond which he tarried a little to look at the city, where subsequently a Stupa was erected, called *Kantaka's Return*. The whole night he rode, reaching in the morning Anupiya on the other side of a great sandy river, Anoma

His marriage, home-life, and indifference.

His great Renouncement.

[10] S. Hardy calls it Golden gate (?), which had stairs. Buddha descended from the doorway of Mâyâdevi's room to the courtyard of the palace and went to the outer gate, page 158. The arched door of his apartment is referred to by Bigandet, I. 61.

(Gandaki ?), and in the country of the Mallas, 12 *yojanas** distant from Kapilavastu. Here he halted in the hermitage of Pokarishi or Bhargavides.

His attainment of Buddha-hood and return to Kapilavastu.

After the attainment of Bodhi (emancipation) at Uruvilva, near Gayâ, 6 years after, and in 103, Anjana era, the Buddha was invited by his father to visit Kapilavastu. He came from Râjgir, which he had entered in the full moon of January with his disciples in the first year of his ministry and in the month of March after the cold season was over, and five months after he had left Benares, where he first preached his doctrines. The distance between Râjgriha and Kapilavastu being 60 *Yojanas*, Buddha leisurely travelled in 60 days.[11] He halted in the grove of Nigrodha,[12] which was a short distance from the town, and which his father dedicated to him and his church. Next day Buddha with his disciples perambulated the streets and begged for food from house to house. The citizens seeing this unusual sight from the different storeys of their houses (*Attâli*) were amazed. On this, Râja Suddhodana came out and took him to the palace, fed him in the upper room, and was converted on hearing his sermon. The crown prince, Nanda, his younger brother, and the son of his step-mother, became his disciple on the very day he was to be made sub-king and married, and renounced a beautiful princess, crown, and kingdom. Buddha's son, Râhula, then 8 years old, also walked in the footsteps of his father; and several citizens followed the example, led by his relatives, Ananda, Anuruddha, and others. The king was mortified to see so many of his family entering the ascetic order, he being left without an heir to his throne. He pathetically protested against this wholesale conversion of his race; and the Buddha was prevailed upon not to initiate any more of the Sâkya youths without their parents' consent. The Buddha returned to Râjgriha *viâ* Anupiya in the country of the Mallas, where Devadatta and other Sâkyas with the barber Upâli at their head entered his order.[13]

Sâkya princes become his disciples.

Buddha pacifies the Sâkyas and the Koliyans.

At a time of unusual drought, the water of the Rohini was shut in by an embankment for the purposes of irrigation; and both the Sâkyas and the Koliyans exclusively claimed it. Hot words passed between the cultivators of the two sides; and soldiers and princes gathered together to support their parties. A battle was imminent, when the Buddha, then at Vaisâli, was informed of it. He came in his 4th *Vas*[14] and pacified the combatants; and thus peace was restored. Buddha converted 500 people on this occasion.

Attends his father's death.

In the middle of the *Vas*, that is, the month of August, the Buddha, while sojourning in Mahâvana monastery near Vaisâli, heard that his father was dangerously ill. He instantly went to Kapilavastu, and attended the last moments of Suddhodana, who was greatly comforted. He breathed his last on the day of full moon of Walchaong, Srâvana, August, on a Saturday at the rising of the sun in the year 107, Anjana era,

---

[11] S. Hardy's *M. B.*, p. 199, says the months were Durutu and Medindina (February, March, and April).

[12] Nigrodha garden was founded by a Sâkya prince of the same name. S. Hardy's *M. B.*, page 200.

[13] This spot was 16 miles from the city, S. Hardy's *M. B.*, p. 281.

[14] *Vas* was derived from the *Sanskrit*, *Varshâ*, the rainy season, and became a technical word meaning the time of Lent or retreat, because the Buddha and his followers then halted at one place, and did not travel to preach and to beg.

* Three *Yojanas* according to Asvaghosha's *Life of the Buddha*, *Sacred Books of the East*, Volume XIX, p. 58.

and at the advanced age of 97 years. The corpse was carried processionally through the principal streets; and the Buddha cremated it on the funeral pile.

Prajâpati, his step-mother, Yasodharâ, his wife, and 500 Sâkya females at this time three times asked his permission to enter his order, but he refused. The Buddha then retired from Nigrodha to Vaisâli, the distance of which was 51 *Yojanas*. There he was followed on foot by the Sâkya and Koliya ladies, who had seldom descended from the upper storeys of their palaces, and who were accustomed to walk on floors made so smooth that they looked like mirrors and reflected the images near them. The soft heart of Ananda, now the constant attendant of the saint, was moved, and he interceded on their behalf. The Buddha at last gave permission for their entering the order; though he observed that admittance of women would not make his institutions last long. In his 8th *Vas*, the Buddha retreated from Srâvasti to Sansumâra-giri (Crocodile hill) in the deer park of Bhesakalâ forest in the Bharga country (or Yaska Bhayankera or Vegga in *Pâli*), which was near Kapilavastu. Here Prince Bodhi had erected a new palace, called Kakanada; where he invited the Buddha to take his meal, and was converted on hearing his doctrines.

Sâkya ladies become nuns.

In the 14th year of his ministry the Buddha visited his native town, when Mahânâma,[14] who had succeeded Bhadraka or Bhaddya, the successor of Suddhodana, became his disciple. He sojourned in the Nigrodha monastery, situated close to the banks of the river Rohini.[15] Among his relatives, Suprabuddha, his father-in-law and maternal uncle, became now his open enemy; and Devadatta, his son, called the son of Godhi (*Vinaya, Chullavarga* VII, Part III, p. 240*) deserted his master, and founded a new sect at Râjgriha under the patronage of Ajâtasatru.

Bhadraka and then Mahânâma succeeds to the Sâkya throne.

The kingdom of Kapilavastu now appeared to be subordinate to that of Kosala and Kâsi. According to the northern version, Mallikâ was the daughter of the Brâhman steward of Mahânâma. On the death of her father, the Râjâ adopted her as his own daughter. She was employed to make garlands of flowers. One day Prasenajit, the king of Kosala, while on a hunting expedition, or as some say while flying after his defeat by Ajâtasatru, came to Mahânâma's garden, and saw her plucking flowers. For her thoughtful kindness, which removed his fatigue, the king asked her from Mâhânama, who said that she was a slave girl, but he can give Sâkya girls better than she. But the king wanted her; and so the lord of Kapilavastu sent her, who was made queen. In course of time she had a son whom the king named Virudhaka. One day Virudhaka went to Kapilavastu and halted at the Santhâgâra, the new assembly hall. It was a large and solid structure with stone pavements, and furnished with pillars, and was erected for the

King Prasenajit of Sravasti marries an adopted daughter of Mahânâma, and had a son, Virudhaka.

---

[14] According to S. Hardy's M.B., p. 227, Mahânâma was the son of Amritodana. Remusat (*Fo Kene Ke*, p. 203) calls Suklodana's sons Bhatrika and Nandaka, and Mani or Aniruddha. Bhaddiya, the friend of Aniruddha, was the Raja of the Sâkyas. Persuaded by the latter, he renounced the world, along with Aniruddha, Ananda, Bhagu, Kimibila and Devadatta with Upâli the barber, and went after crossing (the river) to Anupiya, where Buddha then was (*Chullavarga* 7th *Khundaka*). On this, Mahânâma, the brother of Aniruddha, became king. (*Vinaya* Part III. *Sacred Books of the East*, Volume XX, page 228.)

[15] Near this spot was probably the village of Nigrodhiká, which had a large banian tree that gave shelter to more than five hundred waggons. It was near Kapilavastu, but on the side of the road to Srávasti. Outside the gate of the city, there was a tope close to the banian tree in the park, where he used to walk. Here he was visited by Dandapani, who enquired about his doctrines. The Buddha sometimes sojourned at the Sâkya Vihara of Bamboo wood, and the Kaia Kshamer Vihâra. Yo-la-ti-na (Uradina) was the name of a *Chaitya*, near the Nigrodha-Âsrama, *R. A. S. J.*, p. 519–51 of 1898.

* *Sacred Books of the East*, Volume XX.

reception and preaching of the Buddha. The Sâkyas expelled him, because of his low origin. The young prince thereupon vowed vengeance.

Who usurps the throne.

Shortly after, he usurped the throne of Srâvasti, and his father fled to Râjgir to ask the help of Ajâtasatru, his sister's son, and to recover his kingdom. But on reaching the city he died of cholera.

Attacks the Sâkya capital.

Now Virudhaka, remembering his vow, invaded the Sâkya country; but the Buddha, then at Srâvasti, interceded. The young king returned; but again he issued with his fourfold army, and attacked Kapilavastu; but the Sâkyas fought bravely and repulsed him. At last he prevailed and entered the town at the time of a truce, and began massacring the inhabitants and washing the stone-slabs of the Santhâgâra hall with their blood, exception being made of the family of Mahânâma, the king, who, however, drowned himself in a tank.

Massacres the citizens and sacks the city.

The Sâkyas, who could save themselves, fled in different directions,—some to Nepâl, some to Râjgriha and Vaisâli, some to Vedi, where Asoka long after married the daughter of Sresthi, who gave birth to Mahindra and Samghamitrâ; and others fled to Pippalivana, where the Sâkyas were afterwards known as Mauryas. Virudhaka and Ambarisha, his minister, were burnt to death, a few days after the destruction of Kapilavastu; and Ajâtasatru, the king of Magadha, who was entertaining ambitious designs over the neighbouring kingdoms, invaded the country and conquered both Kosala and Kapilavastu in the 44th year after the attainment of the Buddha-hood.

Ajâtâsatru of Râjgriha conquers Kapilavastu, etc.

The state of Kapilavastu after its sack.

The story of the destruction of Kapilavastu appears to be of an old date, as reference to it is found in "*Vibhâsha-lun*" of Katyâyanaputra and *Avidharma* of Kaniska's council, which quote from an earlier and unknown *Sutra*. When the Buddha visited the desolation of the city, caused by Virudhaka's army, he was ill with a bad headache. But Ananda, who had become his constant companion, from the time when Buddha was 55 years of age, was greatly affected at seeing the city like a cemetery. The walls, houses, doors, and windows were destroyed; and the gardens, orchards, and lotus-ponds were all ruined. The orphaned children followed him with piteous cries for help. Ananda was especially pained to see the mangled bodies of his countrymen, trodden by elephants in the park, near the Sow's tank, close to the Arâma of the Parivrâjaka Tirthikas. Some of the monks had gone to the cold districts of Nepâl, where they were protecting themselves against the frost by the use of *Fulo*, when Ananda visited them. (*R. A. S. J.* for 1898, p. 558-59.)

The city not wholly destroyed.

That Kapilavastu was not, however, altogether destroyed, is proved by the fact, that, the giving of garments to needy brethren, the prohibition against the wearing of ornaments by the Bhikshunis (nuns), and the permission to ordain boys at seven years of age, are all referred to the state of affairs at Kapilavastu immediately after its destruction by Virudhaka. And many Bhikshus seem to have been left uninjured. When the Buddha died at Kusinagara in Anjana era 148—543 B.C., the Sâkyas with an army went there to claim a share of his relics. They brought one-eighth of the Buddha's *Sariras* and erected a Stupa over it. Twenty years afterwards, Kâsyapa, his successor and chief

The Sâkhyas erect a Stupa over Buddha's relics.

of the church, took away some of the relics from here and elsewhere, and collected and buried them in an underground structure at Râjgir. The Mâhâsanghika *Vinaya*, Chapter 30, records a congregation of Bhikshus at the Sâkya city several years after the death of the Buddha, and a feud between Ananda and Râhula on account of an affair connected with a layman's children. This estrangement stopped the regular services of the church for seven years, when the aged Upâli pacified the parties.

It seems from what the Buddha said in his last speech at Kusinagara, that his birth-place at the Lumbini-grove was already held a sacred spot along with those of Bodh-Gayâ, Benares, and Kusinagara, to visit which he recommended his followers.

In course of time the sacred spots of the Buddhists were neglected and forgotten; for the new creed was not yet embraced by the people. Kâlâsoka (or Asoka the Kâkavarna, so called because his colour was very black like a crow), who ascended the throne of Gangetic India in 81 A.B., became a Buddhist through the influence of his sister, Nandi, who was a nun. He assisted the second council at Vaisâli and began patronizing the Buddhistic *Samgha* (church). He also sent for Upagupta at Mathurâ, who was born or initiated in 100 Anno Buddhæ, and became his spiritual guide. With him the king paid pilgrimage to the sacred sites and built, for the guidance of posterity, stone-pillars with inscriptions. The life detailed in *Asokâvadâna* refers more to Kâlâsoka than to Dharmâsoka, who is not known to have paid religious visits to the sacred spots in the Tarai. The dates of Kâlâsoka and Upagupta tally, but the Sthavira of 100 A.B. cannot be contemporary with the king, who began to reign in 218 A.B. Besides, the peculiarities in the short Priyadarsi inscriptions at Niglivâ and Rummin-dei show their age to be earlier than the elaborate edicts at Lowria, Râmpurwâ, Allahabad, and other places. It is not in the natural order of things that the so-called Asoka-Monuments should all be ascribed to a king only,—not one reign before nor one after. Mr. Vincent A. Smith truly remarked in his "Remains near Kasia," page 2, that that emperor has been credited with raising more monuments than it is possible for one sovereign to complete. *Dipavamsa*, Chapter V, expressly records that Asoka was the son of Sisunâga, ruling at Pataliputra; and that Sisunâga was the immediate predecessor of the Nandas.[17]

Kâlâsoka.

At Kapilavastu, Upagupta, with whom Kâlâsoka came here on a pilgrimage in the 21st year of his reign, as recorded in the two pillar inscriptions at Niglivâ and Rummin-dei, pointed out to him many places, some of which were not mentioned by the Chinese pilgrims. The first is the temple of Yaksha (of Iswara, according to Hiuen Tsiang), where the infant Bodhisattva was taken to worship. The next was a Chaitya with representation of Râhulâ and his mother. The third was the schoolroom. Besides these were the spots where king Suddhodana prostrated himself in adoration of the infant Bodhisattva; where Prajâpati nursed the motherless baby; where he excelled all his rivals in the arts of riding, driving, and in the use of arms; and where he enjoyed his family life.

His pilgrimage with Upagupta to Kapilavastu and Lumbinivana. Inscribed pillars erected.

That Kapilavastu rapidly declined after its sack will be evident from stray facts,

[17] The above remarks indicate my views on early Indian history, which I hope to express more fully on another occasion.

gathered from different quarters. In the Ceylonese history (Turnour's *Mahâvansa*, p. 37), we read that Amritodana, the uncle of the Buddha, had seven sons, and a daughter by name Bhadrakânchanâ, who was married to Pânduvâsa, the second king of Ceylon (B. C. 504—474). When she was taken there her seven brothers accompanied her, settling and founding towns in their own names. Their names were Râma, Anurâdha, Uravela, Vijita, Dighâyu and Rohana. Pânduvasa made Vijitapura, founded by Vijita, his capital; while Pandukâbhaya (437—367 B. C.) removed the seat of government to Anurâdhapura, founded by Anurâdha. This Anurâdhapura became the chief city of Ceylon, occupying the most prominent position in the political and ecclesiastical history of the island. The migration of the Sâkyas proves the low state of affairs in Kapilavastu. Dharmapâla, a Buddhist priest of Kapilavastu, went to China, carrying a life of the Buddha, which he translated in 208 A.D., now known in its Chinese garb as *Kung-pen-ki-king*. Buddhabhadra, a descendant of Amritodana, also migrated to China, taking another life of the Buddha, which he translated in 420 A.D.

Fa Hian and Hiuen Tsiang's visit to Kapilavastu.

The decay of Kapilavastu is further proved by the records of the two Chinese pilgrims. Fa Hian, who visited Kapilavastu in about 400 A.D., says that "there is neither king nor people; it is like a great desert. There is simply a congregation of priests and about ten families of lay people." Beal's *Records*, Volume I, p. XLIV.[13] In about 635 A.D. when Hiuen Tsiang paid a visit, he noted that the country, which is about 4,000 *li* in circuit, contains some ten desert cities, wholly desolate and ruined. The capital is overthrown and is in ruins. Its circuit cannot be accurately measured .... It has been long deserted. The peopled villages are few and waste .... There are about 1,000 or more ruined *Sânghârâmas* remaining; by the side of the royal precincts, there is still a *Sânghârâma* with about 3,000 (? 30) followers in it, who study the Little Vehicle of the *Sammatiya* School. Beal's *Records*, Volume II, page 14.

After the period of Hiuen Tsiang, there came to Magadha several pilgrims from China, of whom I-tsing (A.D. 690) is known to have visited Kapilavastu.

Tibetan pilgrims.

The Tibetans appear to have kept a recollection of the Kapilavastu site; and pilgrims used to come here long after the period of Hiuen Tsiang. In a Tibetan guide-book on the sacred sites of the Buddhists, printed in Bengal Asiatic Society's *Journal*, Part III, 1896, it is mentioned that Ganpan, Lalaji, and other Âchâryas visited Kapilavastu; and the religious formula "*Om mane padme Hum*," inscribed on the pillars at Sainâ Mainâ, Rummin-dei, and Nigâli Sâgar, proves that the Tibetans regarded these places with great respect.

Some places not mentioned before.

I may conclude the history of Kapilavastu by mentioning some places, which were not recorded by the Chinese pilgrims and by the author of the *Asokâvadâna*. The eastern boundary of the Sâkya kingdom was a river, called in Chinese books "Aluna" (Aruna). At no great distance from Kapilavastu was the town Nikan (Nigrâma ?), which in some other account is called Mi-chu-hi, that is, the park (Arâma) of the hut

[13] "The country of Kapilavastu is a great scene of empty desolation; the inhabitants are few and far between. On the road the people have to be on their guard against white elephants and lions and should not travel incautiously." Legge's *Fa Hian*, p. 68

"Inside the city, there is neither king nor people; it is just like a wilderness. There are only priests and some tens of families, and that is all." H. A. Giles' *Fa Hian*, p. 49.

of the strayed lord. Kâli was another town of some note, which had a *Vihâra*, where the Sthavira Kâtyayana resided; and where the Buddha once halted and was visited by king Prasenajit. There were other towns of the Sâkyas, namely, Ulumpa, Sâma-gâma, Chatumâ, Metalupa, Khomadussa, a market town, and another, of which the name is rendered in Chinese as "Yellow-pillow." Besides, there were Silâvati, Nava (Chinese Naho), and Karshaka (Chinese Ka-li-sha-ka). The last means ploughing; there Siddhârtha was once sent by his father as Chief Magistrate (*R. A. S. Journal* for 1898, pages 548-49). The Buddha once visited the town Pi-su-na-to, and thence to Kuna or Ko-na, the town of Kanakamuni, while on his way from Kapilavastu to Srâvasti (*R. A. S. Journal*, page 552). Among the mountains of the Sâkya country was one where the aged Asita lived—it was called Kiskindha or Sarvadharâ. The Bell-sound mountain had a village of the family to which Gopâ, Siddhârtha's wife, belonged. (*R. A. S. Journal* for 1898, page 550.)

Chronological Table [1].

Anjana of Devadaba establishes his era in	8640	Kaudza era	=	691	B. C.
Suddhodana born	10	Anjana era	=	681	„
Mâyâdevi „	12	„	=	679	„
Their marriage	28	„	=	664	„
Siddhârtha born	68	„	=	624	„
Do. married . . .	86	„	=	606	„
Do. great renouncement . .	97	„	=	595	„
Do. attainment of Buddha-hood .	103	„	=	589	„
Buddha revisits Kapilavastu in his 1st *Vas*	104	„	=	588	„
Do. attends his father's death in his 5th *Vas*, when Bhadraka became king	107	„	=	585	„
Do. pacifies the Sâkyas and the Kolians in his 4th *Vas* . .	106	„	=	586	„
Bhadraka retires to become a Bhikshu and Mahânâma becomes king . .	107	„	=	585	„
Buddha halts at Sansumâr rock in his 8th *Vas*	111	„	=	582	„
Do. revisits Kapilavastu in his 14th and 15th *Vas*	117-18	„	=	575-74	„
Destruction of Kapilavastu by Virudhaka, son of Parsenajit, king of Kosala, (Sârvasti)	146	„	=	545	„
Mahânâma is drowned; Virudhaka is burned to death.	146	„	=	545	„
Ajâtasatru conquers Kosala, Kâsi, and Kapilavastu	147	„	=	544	„
Buddha's Parinirvâna (death) and the Sâkyas build a *Stupa* over his relics .	148	„	=	543	„
Kâlâsoka's pilgrimage to Lumbini-grâma and Kapilavastu in the 21st year of his reign, and erects the inscribed pillars at Rummin-dei and Niglivâ . . .	102	A. B.	=	441	„
Fa Hian's pilgrimage about . .				405	A. D.
Hiuen Tsiang's do. . . .				637	„
Itsing's do. . . .				690	„

[1] This table represents the views of the author, who accepts the testimony of the Ceylonese and Burmese books as to the date of the death of Gautama Buddha. He believes that this testimony can be reconciled with that of the Jain and Tibetan histories and the archæological evidence. Although I have helped Mr. Mukherji in the preparation of his Report, I have not been able to examine closely his chronological theories, and am not in any way responsible for them, or for any of Mr. Mukherji's opinions. But certainly the current chronology as given in most recent works is by no means convincing. (V. A. Smith.)

Genealogy of the Sâkya royal family.

- Jayasena, king of Kapilavastu.
  - Singhahanu king, (marries Kânchanâ, sister of Anjana.)
    - Mayadevi † } Suddhodana, king † { Prajâpati.
      - (of Mayadevi and Suddhodana) Siddhârtha (Buddha) sub-king, marries Yasodharâ.
        - Râhula.
      - (of Suddhodana and Prajâpati) Nanda, sub-king.
      - (of Suddhodana and Prajâpati) Upananda.
    - (2) Suklodana.
      - Bhadraka or Bhaddiya, king.
      - Ânanda.
    - (3) Amritodana.
      - Mahânâma, king.
      - Anuruddha.
    - (4) Dhotodana.
    - (5) Ghanitadana.
    - (6) Pramitâ.
    - (7) Amrita married to Suprabuddha.
  - Yasodharâ, (married to Anjana of Devadâha.)

Genealogy of the Koliya family.

- Devadâha of Koli.
  - Anjana, marries Yasodharâ.
    - Suprabuddha, marries Amritâ.
      - Devadatta.
      - Yasodharâ, married to Siddhârtha.
    - Dandapâni.
    - Mâyâ. } married to Suddhodana.
    - Prajâpati. }
  - Kânchanâ, married to Singhahanu.

CHAPTER III.

DESCRIPTION OF THE RUINED SITES AT TAULIVÂ, TILAURÂ, AND THEIR NEIGHBOURHOOD.

TAULIVÂ.

TAULIVÂ is the head-quarters of the Provincial Government of Tarai, of which the Subâ is the Commissioner. It is about 7 miles north-west of Piprâvâ, which is near the 44th Boundary pillar, and about 6 miles north of Chândâpar-Shohratgunj, and about 5 miles north of the Boundary pillar, No. 53. It is more like a village than a town, consisting of a large cluster of thatched huts, in the midst of which rises a high temple of Mahâdeva, called Tauliveswara. This is the only brick structure here, and is a land-mark of the country for miles around. It stands on an ancient mound of bricks, and is surrounded by a *Dharmasâlâ*,* where the rich Mahant daily feeds the poor and Sannyâsis. The Dharmasâlâ is built in Nepâlese style; the wall is of bricks; and the gable roof is covered with tiles of the pattern which I discovered in my excavations on the sites of the ancient Pâtaliputra. I noted the manufacture of these tiles by the Nepâlese potters, who use a small framework of bamboo sticks, about 8″ × 4″, and about one inch thick, with another stick below on one side. The lower channel underneath the tile is done by the lower stick, while the upper is done by the finger of the maker at the time of the filling up the framework with prepared mud, mixed with sand. These tiles are afterwards burnt in a kiln. The only difference between the Nepâlese tiles and those I exhumed at Pâtaliputra, is that the latter had holes at one end. In covering the roof, the tiles are placed one over the other, so as to fit the lower channel with the other, and are arranged not straight, but in a rather slanting or diagonal way. This system of ancient tiling, which I could not understand in Behar or Tirhut, and is not known in British territory, is still in vogue in Nepâl,—where, I believe, the lost arts of India are still living in a precarious way.

Manufacture of peculiar tiles.

The courtyard of the Dharmasâlâ, of which the centre is occupied by the temple, is one storey high, being almost flush with the roof of the lower storey. And this high level appears to be made up of the ancient mound, of which the summit was flattened at the time of the building of the temple and Dharmasâlâ. On the east of the temple is a platform, octagonal in plan, where another temple was intended to be raised. On this platform are a few stone fragments of ancient sculpture, and in front of the temple, which is on the north, are the carved jambs of a door. And in the courtyard are several dressed stones, which undoubtedly belonged to an ancient temple, in that material, that must have stood here. The Linga of Mahâdeva, to which the face of Pârvati is attached, appears to be much worn, showing great age. And since it was almost on the road between Rummin-dei (Lumbini grove) and Tilaurâ-koṭ, which I propose to identify with Kapilavastu, this Mahâdeva may be the very Isvara whom the infant Bodhisattva was taken to worship.

Tauliveswara Mahâdeva.

* Hindu sârai, where Sannyâsis and poor people live and are fed for a time.

That Taulivâ was a large site in ancient times will be evident from the extensive ruins on the north side of the village. The village also shows rubble bricks here and there,—undoubted indications of ancient remains. The mounds, or rather elevated fields, on the north, which extend on the west side of the road to Tilaurâ, show unmistakable indications of brick buildings, and in the centre is a mound with ruined walls, on which is a collection of stone fragments of ancient sculpture, worshipped as Samai Mâyi. This mother Samai, who has no place in the authorized Hindu pantheon, appears to be a local and sylvan goddess, particularly presiding over ruined *kots*, and is believed by the people of the Tarai to protect them from all dangers. I doubt not that if excavations are judiciously undertaken here, some very interesting finds may be discovered.

TILAURÂ-KOṬ. (See Plate II.)

Kot or Fort.

The *Kot* or the ruined fort of Tilaurâ is about 2 miles due north of Taulivâ, and is situated on the east bank of the Bângangâ. It is a rectangular fort, about 1,600 feet north to south by 1,000 feet east to west, of which the north-western and south-eastern corners are cut off to form diagonal sides. The north-west portion appears to have been eaten away by the river in ancient times, since when land has formed on that side for a breadth of about 500 feet. Originally it appears to have been a mud fort, on which subsequently brick walls were raised. The mounds of the ruined walls are easily distinguishable on all the four sides. This brick fort was protected by a deep ditch on all sides, as also by a second mud wall and a second but wider ditch.

Fort walls.

On excavating at the sides of the walls on the north and near the eastern gateway I found the breadth to be between ten and twelve feet, having no foundation, and built in mud. This caused the walls to slope on the outside and otherwise to be out of the perpendicular, as shown in Plate II. The size of the bricks in the fort walls is $12\frac{1}{4}'' \times 8'' \times 2''$. On clearing portions of the eastern gate, I found two walls going eastward and at an angle to the main fortification-wall, which goes north to south, and which terminated 10′ 7″ south of the northern cross-wall. Here it extends westward for a length of 17 feet, till a wall appears going southward. Beyond this, the northern wall goes westward again; I do not know how far. 49′ 9″ south of the northern cross-wall is another, also extending eastward. Want of time did not permit me to excavate further and to see whether these two cross-walls formed square bastions by turning outward,—north to south, or innerward, joining the two, to form the outer guard-room of the gate. That there was an inner guard-room is quite plain from what I have exposed already. In front of the gate, that is, on the east, is the vestige of a square structure.

Ruins within the fort.

But before detailing the ruins on the outside of the fort, I describe what are within. The inner area is considerably elevated on the north-western portion, and on the southern half. The southern half is now covered with thick thorny jungle. The northern portion was also full of jungle-trees; but they were removed some twelve years ago by a Sannyâsi, who made this part his hermitage. The northern rampart and the western portion here were still overgrown with thorny vegetation, till I cleared some space for excavation. Beyond the north wall and the ditch the thorny forest is quite impenetrable, where tigers sometimes take shelter. Just on the north of the south wall the inner area is low for about 200 feet, beyond which the ground rises to some height.

On the north-east corner is a tank, which was once large and full of lotus-plants.

Tank on the north-east.

On the west of it is the elevated area, which appears to be the site of the palace. And south of the tank is a low mound, beyond which is a channel that communicates with the eastern ditch and joins the tank by making, on the west, a sweep round a low mound, which is on the south of the tank. On the south of the supposed palace-site is another tank, now almost filled up and dry. And the ground extending eastward from this tank to the east gate is comparatively low.

I mentioned before that the western wall, which goes from the north-western corner towards the south, was cut away in some unknown age. The débris of the northern half of this wall cannot, therefore, be traced down to where the western gate stood. The palace area proper is consequently not now large.

Palace-site and excavation.

In the middle of this site is a modern temple, presumably raised on an ancient foundation, which is dedicated to the sylvan deity called Samai Mâyi, represented by a small collection of stone fragments of ancient sculpture.

Samai Mâyi.

Minutely examining the mounds, I began excavation on the west and east of the small temple in the shape of two trenches from north to south.

See Plate III.

And though several walls were removed by the Sannyâsi to get bricks for his hut, as the lines of the hollows showed, I succeeded before long in exposing a number of walls, for which purpose I had not to go below five feet.

Walls exposed: original masonry.

Some of these walls appeared to be raised after the decay of the original edifices; and the foundation walls of the original monuments were traced much below those built in subsequent periods. The original structure, of which a good specimen was unearthed on the west of the modern temple, proved to be very neat masonry, in bricks, of course, set in mud; but the bricks are so smoothly jointed that the lines of the courses are not easily visible even at a short distance. The subsequent masonry is more rough and inartistic.

About 25 feet west of this original masonry, I exhumed another structure, whose walls were traced on three sides,—south, west and north; and on the east was cleared the concrete and lime pavement, whose composition is interesting in its way.

A structure with concrete flooring.

Another pavement was discovered about two feet below in another trench I dug north-west of the modern temple. The walls of the western building showed covered bricks in the plinth line and elsewhere, but not in any design or system, which fact proved it to be not a part of the original building.

On the east of the modern temple of Samai Mâyi, several walls were exposed, showing structures of sorts. But want of time did not allow me to complete the excavations here. I could not, therefore, fully trace out the buildings. Of these, two, however, I completely traced round; one was an octagonal structure, probably a Stupa, and the second a square building.

Two other monuments, square and octagonal.

A wall, in continuation of the western walls of the two structures, went considerably southward.

Since, almost at first sight, I thought that Tilaurá-koṭ might represent the ancient and now forgotten Kapilavastu, and the north-west mound, the site of the palace, it struck me as very possible that the mound north-east of the latter, might conceal a Stupa,—that of Asita,—as mentioned by Hiuen Tsiang. Accordingly, I excavated here,

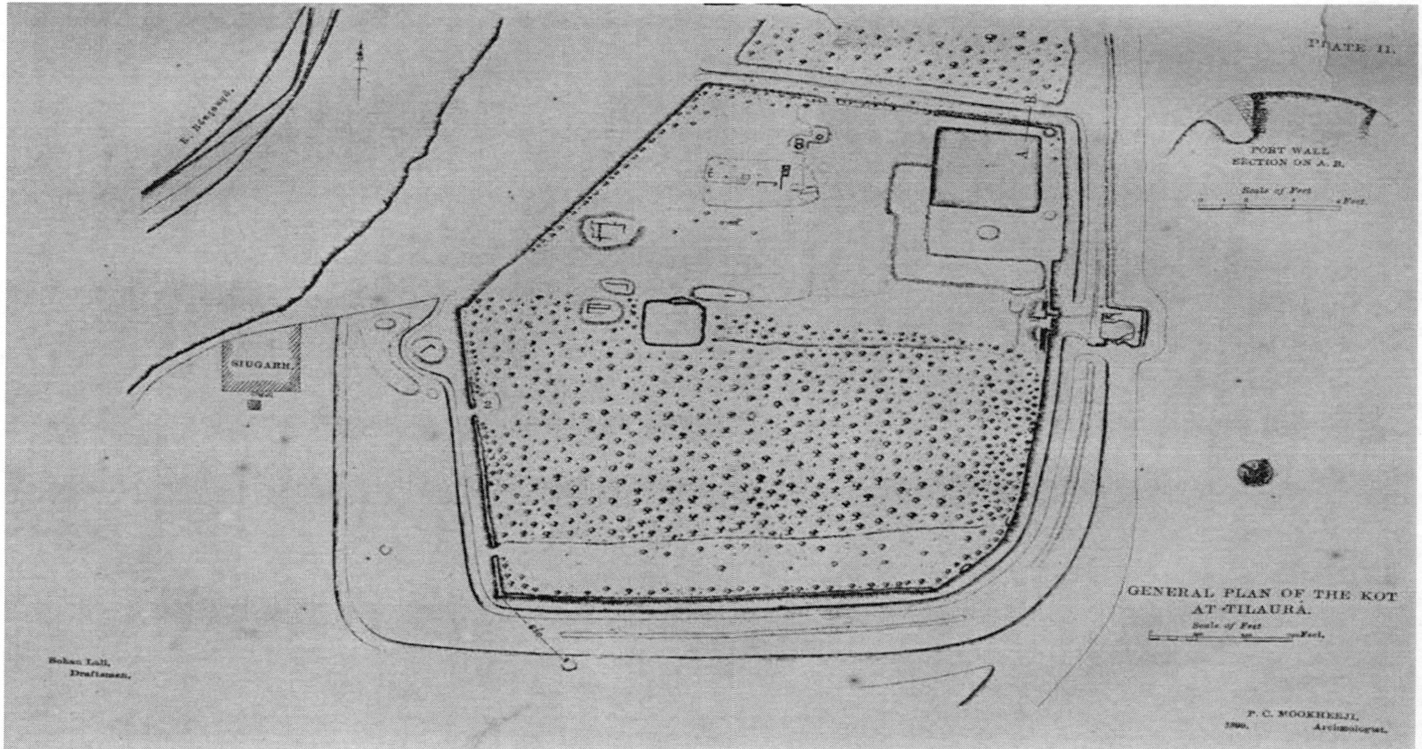
PLATE II.
FORT WALL
SECTION ON A. B.
Scale of Feet
SIUGARH
GENERAL PLAN OF THE KOT
AT TILAURĀ.
Scale of Feet
Sohan Lall,
Draftsman.
P. C. MOOKHERJI,
Archæologist.

and, before long, two structures were found—one 16-sided and the other square with rectangular projection in the middle of each side. The 16-sided structure, which is south-west of the other, had an additional wall on the north to form, most probably, the portico. It appeared to be of solid brick-work,—unmistakable indication of a Stupa, which fact showed that my surmise was correct. North of the square structure, the mound extends and shows that it was made up of rubble-bricks; though time did not allow me to clear it completely, so as to trace out the hidden monument minutely. About 100 feet north of this was the northern gate of the fort.

Two other structures, cruciform and sixteen-sided in plan.

Returning to the central tank, mounds are visible at some distance on the west, north, and south-east. And on the north-west, that is, south-west of the modern temple, is a large mound, which, on superficial excavation, yielded a building of respectable dimensions. But it was not completely opened. The mound on the west of the tank showed another structure, of which the plan is square and the northern room long and narrow. On the mound on the north of the tank, vestiges of brick buildings were exposed on superficial excavation. The mound on the south-east of the tank showed indications of buildings, a portion of the wall being exposed on the west, which extended towards south-west.

Central tank and mounds.

On the south of these ruins the fort area is covered with jungle; and though it is elevated, I could not detect brick remains or rubbles scattered about, which fact showed that this part of the citadel was occupied with mud and *kalcha* houses.

Jungles and gates on the southern area of the fort.

On the southern wall of the citadel there appeared to be a gateway on the south-east. But in the middle there was a second gate, which is now not easily distinguishable from the line of débris. North of this wall and parallel to it, the inner area is low, for about 200 feet, which opens towards the west wall, where was a gate, as proved by the line of the western wall breaking here. About 500 feet north of this there is another break in the western débris of wall, which shows that another gate was here.

Now, returning to the east gate and going out about 50 feet, I found the remains of a large and square building, of which vestiges of walls were traced on the north and south.

East gate and an out-house.

The original walls, after their fall, were very badly restored afterwards, as shown by the portions being out of perpendicular and right angle. That fact showed the precarious existence of the inmates at a period subsequent to the original structure. The existence of a building just in front of the gate of a fort, which weakened and interfered with its capabilities for defence, proved that this out-house was built when the citadel ceased to be the abode of the Râjâ; and hence no longer served the purpose of defence. The fact appears to be that it was constructed, when the fort was in ruins, as its very masonry showed.

About 600 feet south-east of the east gate is a large mound, which, on first inspection, I detected to be a Stupa. Before my arrival here, the Nepâlese had, at the request of Major Waddell, cut a trench without finding anything. I changed the direction of the excavation; and the same day, a portion of the circular structure was laid bare on the

Stupa.

See Plate IV.

north-east. Digging also on the west, south, and east, I found the circumference, which I then measured and drew. It appears to be made up of several concentric circles of large bricks; and the circular platform for the purpose of circumambulation appeared to have been once paved with concrete. The different sizes of the bricks in the several parts of the structure showed the different ages of the building—those of the largest size belonging to the inner and original structure. On minutely examining the trench from north to south, or rather from north-east to south-west, I found that the northern portion of the Stupa, south of the platform, was excavated in some unknown age, presumably for the purpose of removing the relics. While I was absent at Sâgarwâ Major Waddell ordered, on 20th February last, the centre of the Stupa to be dug deep down to the very soil, before he left the place. The hole, about 11 feet deep and 10 feet in diameter, did not bring to light any relics or bones as I had supposed before,—for ages ago the Stupa was opened a little on the northern side. I took minute measurements and a plan with section of the Stupa before I filled up the excavations.

The position of the Stupa in relation to the eastern gate struck me as having some meaning, presumably associated with the life of the Buddha. Beyond the Stupa and a short distance on the south-east was a large tank, now dry, south of which is another tank, not less ancient, which is on the west of Sandwâ. The outer ditch on the east branches southwards at the south-east corner, where it turns towards the west, on the south of the fort. It then forms a rivulet during the rains and going west of Taulivâ joins a river in British territory. Was it the missing Rohini?

Two large tanks and the outer ditch forming a rivulet.

On the north of the citadel, and the northern inner ditch, is another and triangular plot of high ground, now covered with impenetrable jungle, which, no doubt, formed an inhabited part of the ancient town. The outer ditch turns round this plot on the north to go towards the west.

Mounds on the north of the Kot.

On the west, and going up from the south-west corner, the outward ditch extends to the village of Sheugarh, on the north of which the ground slopes down considerably to the upper bed of the Bângangâ. Now, from the western gate of the citadel to another, which I mark on Plan as No. 2, and beyond the inner ditch, extends a semicircular piece of mound, of which the northern portion is high, where probably was a Stupa in mud. And in the centre of this semicircular area is a comparatively high ground, where on excavation I exhumed the brick foundation of a large room, a *vihâra*—probably of ancient times. On the west of this, the inner ditch makes a semicircular sweep to pass towards the north.

A Vihâra and mounds on the west of the Kot.

On the west of the probable site of the gate No. 2, and beyond the inner ditch, is a small eminence made of yellowish earth, where probably was once a Stupa.

On the south of the southern ditch is a mound of earth, where is scattered a large amount of iron refuse, or something like it, which shows that there was a large workshop here in ancient days. The mound is surmounted by a large tree. About 100 feet west of it is an ancient well. About 600 feet south of it is another. In the village of Derwâ, about two furlongs south, are an ancient tank and the ruins of two Stupas, or something very like them.

Mounds on the south.

That the ancient town extended a long way on the north, east, and south, of the *Kot*, will be known by the extent of high ground from Râmghât to the two village of Tilaurâ.

CHITRÂ-DEI. (See Plate V.)

That the city, of which the Koṭ at Tilaurâ was the central citadel, was of large size, will be evident from the extensive ruins at Chitrâ-dei, which occupied the western side of the river and were undoubtedly of contemporary origin. Chitrâ-dei (Devi) is literally the goddess Chitrâ, from whom the name of the village is derived, and who is still worshipped, with terracotta elephants, in a few fragments of ancient sculpture, consisting of a Linga, a headless bust, and a third, which cannot be distinguished. These fragments, with a number of the elephant-dolls, are now on a small mound of ancient temple, of which the platform wall is still traceable, that on the south side having been removed by some villagers of old.

Chitrâ-dei.

Crossing the river and going about two furlongs west, the ground rises considerably, which extends from north-east to south-west. This, most probably, was the ancient and outer bank of the river. Going up to the high bank from the south-east and crossing the remains of a boundary wall, the first mound that one sees is a small one, of which the western and northern wall I partly excavated. Inside the shrine I cleared and found it to be 5′-4½″×5′-2″, of which the corners were occupied by pilasters, about 5″×4″ in section. The back wall was 4′-6″ in breadth, while in the front wall, in the east, was the door, 3′-6″ in breadth. The double stone pedestal, one over the other, of which the upper one has a hole on the upper surface for fitting in the image of the presiding deity—now gone—is 2′-9″ long by 1′-6″ broad, and about 1′-6″ in height. These two pedestals show the usual mouldings and recessing. A fragment of a *Ganeśa's* head was discovered among the rubbish. The back wall, of which a small portion remains, showed coursing in projecting-bricks. Misunderstanding my instructions to clear the shrine, the Nepâlese dug a deep hole in the centre, which showed solid brick-work down to 7′-6″, when I stopped this destructive digging. I do not know how far down this solid brick-work went. About 2 feet below the pedestal stone a concrete pavement was visible, which fact showed that the original temple had its floor much below the later one, where the double pedestals of the image of probably Ganeśa were fixed, presumably when the original structure decayed and another was built over it.

A temple—probably of Ganeśa.

Seventy-six feet west of the Ganeśa temple is a well, now filled up with rubbish; and about 85 feet north is a very small mound, which I did not examine by digging. Two hundred and forty feet north is the largest of the Chitrâ-dei mounds, where I excavated to a large extent and brought to light the biggest of ancient temples I yet discovered in the Tarai. Two hundred and sixty-eight feet north of this large mound is another of smaller size. One hundred and eleven feet east of the last is the platform of Chitrâ-dei goddess, 14′-9″ long × 7′-6″ broad, where are the three stone fragments and a number of terracotta elephants mentioned before. Seventeen feet and nine inches south is a well, now filled up and dry. Three hundred and fifty feet east of Chitrâ-dei temple is a brick structure, from which bricks in large quantities have been taken out by the villagers, leaving a

Outer mounds.

deep hole. Beyond this, again, was another room, of which the four walls are traceable. Between Chitrâ-dei and the excavated building is another mound a little towards the north.

On the north of the westernmost mound, the high ground extends to a length of about 500 feet. A sort of channel is on the west of the mound, which goes from south to north, and, turning eastward and then southward, again extends eastward to the edge of the ancient bank; and thus encloses the mounds on the north side. On the south of the Ganeśa mound, the boundary wall extends from west to east and then turns north-east, thus making a sort of a fortified place with the ditch on the west and north, and the river on the south-east. But the town extended beyond this, both on the north-east and south-west in the line of the ancient banks.

The big mound and a magnificent temple exhumed.

Returning now to the biggest mound, which I closely examined, I began excavation on the 25th February last. Observing a hollow on the south, where bricks from the existing walls were removed several years before, I employed the diggers here. A wall about 4 feet broad was traced for a length of about 40 feet from east to west, where the thick roots of a big tree stopped further excavation. At the eastern end, the wall turned northward; but here the bricks have been removed. Continuing the excavations on other sides in the lines of the cross-walls that began appearing as the work progressed, I found the whole structure to be rectangular, about 51′-6″×45′, with rectangular projections 22′× about 14′, in the middle of all sides; so that the plan appeared to be cruciform with minor projections in the angles. These projections, one in advance of another, are known in *Silpa-Sástras* I discovered at Puri, Orissa, in 1892, as *Rathakas*, which I may translate as bays. Now, a plan having seven *Rathakas*, as this great structure shows, is called *Saptaratha*. There were several rooms, of which the central one, which is about 13 feet broad by about 46½ feet long, appeared to be the most important. Its inner wall showed recesses; and the doors were in both sides, west and east, occupying the middle of the long walls. The inner area is full of masses of concrete, which evidently belonged to flat roofs. Among these concrete masses, were found a few pieces of lime plaster, which showed that the rooms were whitewashed and coloured in the borders.

See Plates V and VI.

Ornamented plinth existing.

See Plate VI, Fig. 1.

But the most interesting of the remains here is the plinth of the ancient monument, which appeared to be once a magnificent temple in its original construction. The existing plinth is about 7 feet still in height. The lower wall rises to about 2′-2″ in three receding courses, crowned by a half torus (*Kumbha*) to join the lower neck. These two courses of bricks project to 2½″, above which the third course shows receding by about 3 inches, and forms the lower portion of the big cyma. Above three courses of bricks, of which the middle one is a sort of *Galá* or necking, projects a torus (*Kumbha*) of three bricks; over that is a course of one brick, of which the upper portion shows a small cyma. Above this, again, is another neck (*Galá*), surmounted by a course projecting about an inch. Then comes up another neck, over which is another course, that boldly projects from below to up in the form of a cyma (*Padma*). Now from the lower Padma to the upper, which occupies a height of about 2′-6″, the whole length of each *Rathaka* is broken and relieved by projecting mouldings, two in number, in the temple-form, and three smaller and triangular ones, the latter occupying the line of the lower cyma.

These projecting mouldings are pretty in design, of which the middle portion is in prominent relief, having the edges in parallel lines with the outer form. Above them the plinth wall rises to 1′-3″ receding in three courses. Then the uppermost courses show projections, of which one has cyma; above that is a sort of dentils done by the bricks being laid diagonally and one corner being exposed. Two more courses of single bricks project one over the other, and thus make up an elaborate plinth. Innumerable carved bricks in different sizes and designs showed how magnificently the superstructure must have been built. Innumerable iron nails were found, which were rusty with age. They were about 3″ long with a knob above. The roofing, which appeared to be flat and not like the *Śikhara* form, was done in concrete, about 6″ in thickness, above which plaster, about 2″ thick, was laid. The walls of the inner rooms showed recesses at short distances; and in the corners were pilasters, most probably of wood, which must have decayed in the course of ages, leaving empty spaces. Had there been stone pilasters, some vestiges must have been found. Want of time did not permit me to clear the whole structure nor the inner areas of the rooms, hence I did not find any vestiges of the presiding image of this temple, the access to which was from the east, where on the projecting *Rathaka* was the flight of steps, rising in two stairs, one from the north and the other from the south. It should be completely cleared before we can form an adequate idea of this magnificent temple in the land of the Sâkyas.

Sohangarh and Changât Deviki Sthân.

Sohangarh is about 6 *kos* (12 miles) north-west of Chitrâ-dei on the way to Śiugarhi, a temple of Śiva crowning the peak of the lower Himâlayas. Here is a fort and several ruins with some stone images, of which one is unbroken. Changât is about 10 miles (5 *kos*) on the north of Chitrâ-dei, where the temple of the Devi has its wall still standing, the goddess, I was informed, being a piece of unbroken sculpture of ancient times. These two places are hidden in the forest, and I could not find time to visit them.

Sâgarwâ. [See Plate VIII.]

About two miles north of Tilaurâ-koṭ and embedded in the dense and thorny jungle, is a large ancient tank, known as Sâgar—1,059′×225′. It is about two furlongs east of Bânganga and the village of Sâgarwâ, the name of which is derived from the tank. About 120 feet west of the tank, is a high mound, which two years ago the Nepâlese had excavated and exhumed an ancient building. Last year when Dr. Führer was here, this monument was further excavated and a structure of twelve rooms, each about 9′×10′ with very thick walls and planned in the form of a cross, was brought to light. The walls are very broad, being between 6′ and 4′ thick, and still about 15′ high. No door or opening was visible in the walls of the rooms. Attached to the western wall of this monument was a solid structure in brick, whose superstructure was probably in the form of a Stupa. Its lower portion existed up to about 15 feet. About 15 feet below the summit of the solid brick-work, which was removed, a plan of 49 squares was exposed. A tank, about 5 feet deep and 35½′ square, was excavated; and then a smaller tank, 15′ square and 3′ deep, was cut

Sâgar.

A cruciform monument attached to a Stupa.

See Plate IX.

See Plate X.

through the solid brick-work. In the centre was found a single earthenware casket, of which the lid was of copper. This casket contained bones, two triangular bits of gold and silver, two Nâgas in gold, greenish crystals, a ruby, talc, and a few grains of rice. It is extremely to be deplored that so much destructive work has been done in the name of archæology. When I arrived there, I could not see what the Doctor described; but instead found a small tank in the midst of a deeper and bigger one on the west of the structure from the walls of which bricks are now removed by the villagers.

Relics found in a casket.

About 200 feet east of the monument was a long row of small Stupas, which Dr. Führer described as square. But I very much doubt the existence of square Stupas, for, since their superstructure was in ruins, the square basement cannot prove that they were square above. Stupas commonly rise from a square basement, and then form the drum and the hemisphere. What I saw is a long series of small tanks in a deep hollow extending about 350 feet southward and about 70 feet west of the tank. About 220 feet south of the tank is another long hollow, caused by last year's excavations, which extended 250 feet further southward. About 320 feet south of the so-called Vihâra was another Stupa, 33′×25′, marked '2,' in the plan, and about 200 feet further south is a room 83½′×32⅞′. About 25 feet west of the big Stupa, which had inside 49 subdivisions, are two plots of excavated areas, where was found the corner of a room, on the south of which are two small Stupas. On the north also are some ruins embedded in the ground. About a furlong further north are remains of brick structures on the way from Sâgarwâ to Bandauli.

Row of small Stupas on the east of Stupa.

Other excavated ruins.

Now, returning to the excavated area on the west of the tank, I found traces of about seven small Stupas, which have been completely dug out, leaving small tanks full of water. In the absence of records I referred to the draftsman, Babu Bhairava Buksh, who drew the seventeen Stupas last year, while being destroyed, and who has numbered them from memory. About 700 feet south-east of these and about 220 feet south of the tank the hollow showed marks of nine Stupas.

Destructive excavation of last year.

The dimensions of the bases of these 17 Sâkya Stupas, which have been thus removed from the face of the earth, were not uniform. The largest, No. 9, for example, was about 19 feet square, while the smallest, No. 12, was about 3 feet only. No. 7, which was 10½′ square, was 8¾′ in height. These Stupas were built of well-burnt bricks, which measured 11″×7″×1½″ and were laid in clay. At the level of the foundations the last layer consisted of nine, seven, or five bricks, each carved in the design of a full-blown lotus, under which the relic-caskets were found embedded in the soil.

Formation and size of the 17 Stupas.
See Plate XI.
" XII.
" XIII.

Now to give details of the finds of the Stupas:—I may commence with No. 1, which was 4⅞′×4¼′. Removing all the bricks, Dr. Führer came down upon the last course or layer of bricks, which consisted of five laid in the level of the earth, and of which the four on the outside showed marks of a cross. The ends of the cross were turned on the left. The fifth brick in the middle had a circular hole in the centre of the upper surface,

Stupa No. 1.

PLATE VIII

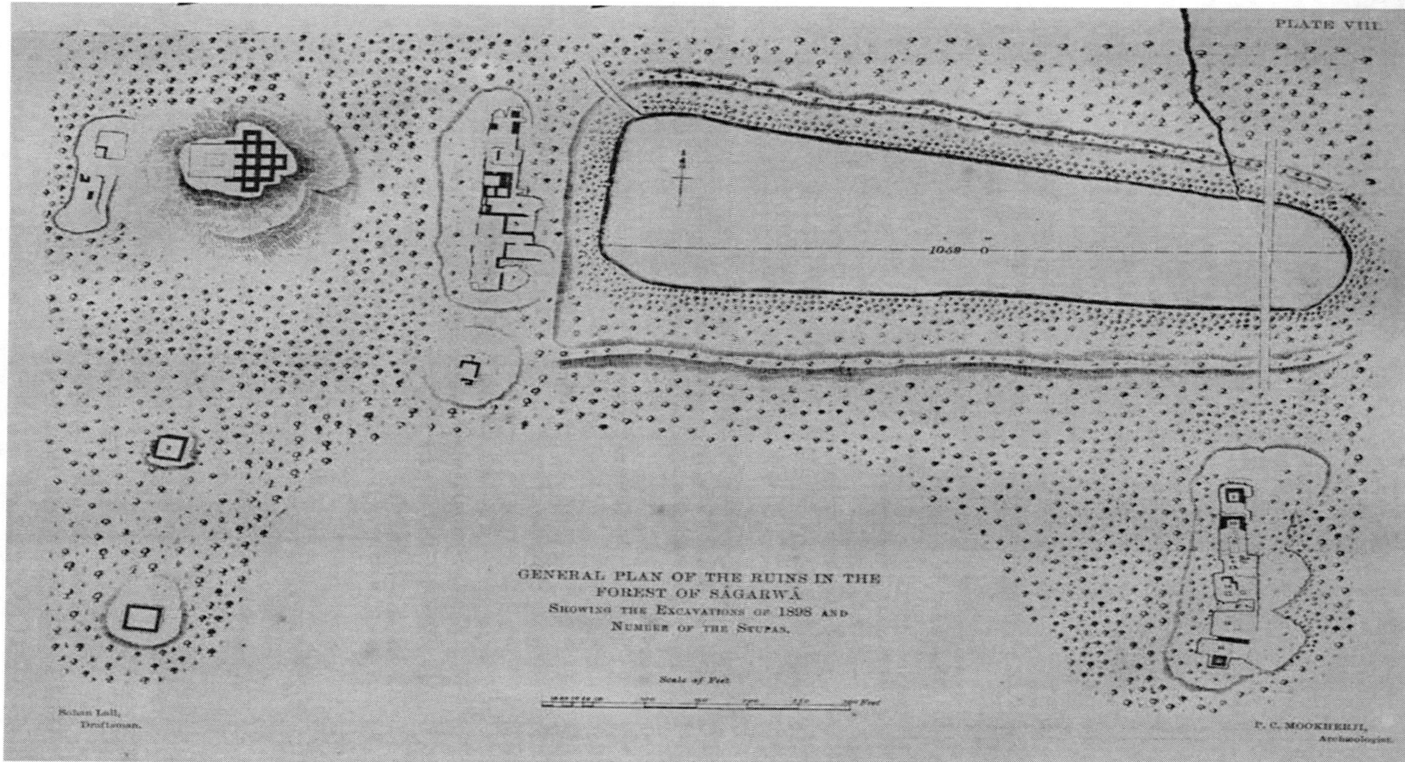

GENERAL PLAN OF THE RUINS IN THE FOREST OF SĀGARWĀ
SHOWING THE EXCAVATIONS OF 1898 AND NUMBER OF THE STUPAS.
Scale of Feet
1059
Sohan Lall, Draftsman.
P. C. MOOKHERJI, Archaeologist.

Above this central brick was another, which had the carving of a lotus-flower. The relic-casket was found below the brick with the lotus.

No. 2, which was 17′×16′ in size, had, in the last layer of bricks (each 10½″×7½″)

No. 2.

four *Swastika* (cross) in the four corners, and in the central one, a lotus, of which the centre showed a hole. Below this central brick and in the level of the earth, was found a relic-casket containing two Nâgas and four pieces of silver and gold.

No. 3, which was 10¾′×10¼′ in size, yielded a casket below a carved brick. The

No. 3.

casket was of the usual pattern, in which ten relics were found; in one leaf was what looked like a seated human figure and in another an animal.

No. 4, which was 15′×15½′ in size, appeared to be very rich in yielding relics. In

No. 4.

the central hole of a brick carved with lotus were found the relics. A large lotus in a leaf covered the hole of the brick, underneath which were found a Nâga and six other relics of sorts.

No. 5, size 17½′×17½′, showed, in the lowest layer, 5 bricks having carvings of

No. 5.

lotus, one being in the centre and four in the north-east, north-west, south-west and south-east. Below these were found five relic-caskets.

No. 6, size 16¾′×16¼′, showed, in the lowest stratum, bricks, of which the eight

No. 6.

outer ones exhibited symbols of Trisula (trident), dagger, arrow, etc. The brick, covering the relic-casket, showed the usual lotus done in a square.

No. 7, size 10½′×10¾′, and before excavation, was 8½′ in height. No relic appears

No. 7.

to have been found here.

No. 8, size 14½′×15¼′, showed 9 bricks in the lowest stratum, all exhibiting devices

No. 8.

with the exception of the central one, on which is carved a lotus, circular in design, below which was found the relic-casket. It contained seven relics.

No. 9, size 19′×19′, showed 9 bricks in the lowest stratum. The eight outer bricks

No. 9.

showed different kinds of ancient weapons and the central brick a lotus, below which was found the casket with five relics.

No. 10, size 17¾′×17½′, showed, in the lowermost layer, a single and square brick

No. 10.

carved with lotus, above which is another layer of three bricks marked with signs. Above this again, were four bricks, also figured with Trisulâ, dagger, etc.

No. 11.

No. 11, size 13½′×13½′, appeared to have yielded no relics.

No. 12.

No. 12, size 12¼′×12¼′, yielded three caskets below a covered brick.

No. 13, size 15½′×15½′, showed five bricks in the lowest stratum, of which the four

No. 13.

outer ones showed cross, trident, dagger, and disc, and the central one lotus, below which was found a beautiful casket in bronze. It contained three relics.

No. 14.

No. 14, size 16'×15¼', had the lowest brick carved in lotus and another brick of peculiar shape having a knob in a circular hole and a clay casket.

No. 15.

No. 15, size 11'×12', had ten bricks in the lowest stratum, of which five were carved with lotus, yielding from below two relic-caskets.

Nos. 16 and 17.

No. 16, size 7¾'× 7⅓'
No. 17, size 11¾'×12' } These two do not appear to have been fully excavated, and so did not yield any relics.

Besides what are detailed above I could not find any other mounds either in the thick forest or in the open, though I walked several times and in different directions. About half-a-mile south of the big Stupa is the village of Srinagar, on the west of which the ground is high on two sides of an ancient channel now dry. And on the north of the village is an ancient tank.

"Place of Massacre of the Sâkyas."

The rows of Stupas were identified by Dr. Führer as the "Place of Massacre of the Sâkyas" mentioned by the Chinese pilgrim Hiuen Tsiang, as being situate several *li* on the north-west of Kapilavastu, which the Doctor locates somewhere here.

Dr. Führer's identification of Kapilavastu unsatisfactory.

The outer boundary of Kapilavastu was described by him as Jagadispur and Bikuli on the north, Srinagar, Ahirauli, and Râmapur on the east, and Śiugurh and Râmghât on the south. At the same time, he locates the south gate of the capital somewhere near Srinagar. If the city extended some 3 miles south of Srinagar, how could the south gate be fixed here at a point, which, according to him, was evidently the middle of the eastern side? And if the place of massacre or battle-field was several *li* north-west of the city, how can it occupy its very centre? And if the Bikuli temple was the very shrine of the Isvara, where the infant Bodhisattva was taken on his way from Lumbini to the city, it cannot form the north-west boundary line, for it should be some distance from the city and on the south-east and not north-east. In fact, Dr. Führer's identifications are full of contradictions. In the region, consisting of several villages, mentioned by him, I could not detect any ruins, except those at the Sâgarwâ forest, Bikuli, and in the jungle about two furlongs west of Ahirauli. No ruins have been found in any other villages. I cannot, therefore, understand how he could extend the city over so many villages and determine its central point in such erroneous and contradictory fashion.

Bikuli. (See Plates XIV and XV.)

About 3 miles east and a little north of Sâgarwâ, and on the outskirts of the forest, is situated the Thâru village of Bikuli. On the north of it the ground considerably slopes down. About a furlong north-west of the village and in the low ground is a large and ancient tank; on the south and west of which

A tank and embankment.

extend two mounds of the embankments at right angles to one another. On the summit of the western mound some brick ruins were visible, and last year Dr. Führer, who called it Kotahi-kot, had it excavated in a most unskilful way. His usual procedure

A fine temple destroyed.

was to dig a tank and then to search for the remains. In this way the diggers destroyed much brick masonry before they were detected and stopped. Three-fourths of the principal temple was thus dug out from the very foundation on the northern side, leaving only a small portion on the south face. In the same way portions of the other two temples were broken. The excavated area, about 125′ × 50′, is now full of water, eating away the mud cement of the existing brick masonry, which is thus undermined and falling in masses. The largest of the three temples had some interesting features. Its shrine was octagonal in plan, of which each side was broken and relieved by receding lines, the junction of the diagonal sides being hollowed into triangular recesses. The stone drain with the Makara's head was on the north side, communicating from the centre, where stood the Linga.

Lingas and carved stones.

Here were found a few more Lingas, presumably brought in from the other temples, when they decayed. Here were seen two stone capitals, which were carved, and which proved that the inner room had pilasters in the corners. Here was also found a stone *Nandi*, Siva's bull. About 25 feet north-west of it, was a second temple, $14' \times 13\frac{1}{2}'$, octagonal in plan, of which the diagonal walls are built in recesses.

Another temple octagonal in plan.

The third temple is $78\frac{2}{3}'$ to the north of the first. It is $9\frac{1}{2}'$ square. The basement is $2\frac{1}{2}'$ high. Then receding about 6″ the plinth rises to about 10,″ above which the wall is constructed in carved bricks, and of which about $1\frac{1}{4}'$ in height remains. Above the plinth the plan is reticulated into a *Saptaratha*, receding in rectangles one behind the other.

A third temple, Saptaratha.

On the west of the octagonal temple the enclosure wall extends to 18′ and then turns southward, where about $67\frac{1}{2}'$ was traced. On the south of the northern temple were other structures, of which even the plinths are gone. And $22\frac{1}{4}'$ on the east of the octagonal temple is a portion of brick wall. Between the largest temple and the western boundary wall is another mass of masonry; and in the south are other brick-works, all of which should have been skilfully traced for the purpose of accurate drawing.

The multitude of carved bricks, in innumerable patterns, that are scattered about the place, proved that the superstructures were highly ornamented; and the few stones carved in ornamental designs must have belonged to a temple, which was undoubtedly built in that material.

Wrong identification again.

Dr. Führer identifies the largest temple as that of Abhayâdevi, the goddess of the Sâkyas, where the infant Bodhisattva was brought on his way from Lumbini to Kapilavastu. But the name Abhayâ is not found in *Lalita Vistâra*, where Siva and other gods of the Brahmanical pantheon are mentioned. And Hiuen Tsiang records him as Isvara, that is, Mahâdeva, the great god Siva. If Abhayâdevi be the same as Parvati, I could not find any figure or fragment of her amidst a number of Lingas and other sculptures. And how could she rise in a bent position—a sculptural phenomenon—I could not see or understand. The fact is that the temple cannot be identified with that of Isvara; as not only it stood out of the way, but Bikuli did not form the eastern or any boundary of Kapilavastu, of which the vast and immense ruins, that the Doctor said would occupy the Archæological Survey for several years, I could not trace anywhere.

NIGÂLI SÂGAR.

Nigâli is a village about a mile-and-half east of Sâgarwâ and on the east of the local forest. About a mile south of the village is a large tank extending east to west, which is known as Nigâli Sâgar from the two portions of a Priyadarsi pillar, called Loriki-Nigâli or smoking-pipe, which are in the western embankment. The embankments on all sides, especially on the north, are still very high. They appear to have subsequently been restored at the time of the re-excavation of the tank. The other tanks in the neighbourhood show their banks almost flush with the surrounding ground level.

Nigâli tank.

Priyadarsi pillar.

The Nigâli Sâgar is now shallow. The upper piece of the pillar, which lies fallen inside the embankment and just above the water in February, is about 14′-9½″ long, the upper girth being 6′-6″ and the middle is 6′-10¼″; and the diameters at the top and the bottom are, respectively, 2′ and 2¼′. There are three birds of a very rude pattern done in some mediæval times, when the pillar was fallen. Between 8′-6″ and 9′-7″ below the top are two short inscriptions in four lines, the upper two being the Tibetan creed "*Om mani padme hum,*" translated "O! the jewel is in the lotus," and the lower, "Sri Tapu Malla Jayastu—Sambat 1234," "May Tapu Malla be victorious,—A. D. 1177-78."

See Plate XVI, Figs. 7 and 4.

The top of the pillar has a diameter of 2′, above which a smaller drum rises 2½″. In the centre of this is a hole, 4″ in diameter, and 1′-4″ in depth, in which was fitted the copper mortice of the capital, that is now missing. The lower portion of the pillar is about 10′, on the top of the western embankment. Its upper diameter is 2′-4″, and the girth, at 2′-4″ below top, is 7′-5½″. The inscription, in four lines, which occupies 1′-4″, below the top, records in ancient *Pâli* that "King Priyadarsi, beloved of the gods, having been anointed 14 years increased for the second time the Stupa of Budha Kanakamuni and having been anointed (20 years) he came himself and worshipped: (and) he caused (this stone pillar to be erected)." Some of the letters are gone with the lower faces, leaving only a length of 7′-7½″ to the bottom, now broken off.

Inscription.

The pillar is not *in situ;* for Dr. Führer was mistaken in saying so. When Major Waddell excavated below, the broken bottom was exposed, where no foundation or basement was discovered. Nor could I find the Stupa of Konâgamana, which, according to the Doctor's statement, was at a short distance from the western embankment, where he located "vast brick ruins stretching far away in the direction of the southern gate of Kapilavastu." Standing on the summit of the western embankment, I could see for a mile or two westward to and beyond Râmapur, Abhiauli, and Srinagar; and I have walked over the tract in different directions; but nowhere could I see such an enormous pile nor was I informed of it. In fact, the alleged Stupa is not in existence.

Konâgamana's Stupa not in existence.

I saw some large tanks, now very shallow with age, which are in the east and north of the village at Râmapur. This proves that there was a small town here in ancient times. The banks around the tanks have all been washed down by the rains of ages,—so much so that they could be hardly distinguished from the surrounding level country.

ARAURÂ-KOT. (See Plate XVI—Fig. 5.)

The Kot at Araurâ Mouzâh is about 1,500 feet south-east of the Nigâli Sâgar between which flows the rivulet Jâmuâr. It is a rectangular fort, about 750′×600′. Its walls on the north and west were of mud, while those on the east and south were of bricks, about 12′ broad and still about 15′ in height. In the middle of the eastern and western walls were the two gates, giving access to the inside. This fort was protected by a ditch, which surrounded it on all sides, and which is still deep on the south side. On the east it is double, to make that side additionally strong, more so as there were two more walls of earth. One was between the two ditches, and a third outermost on the outer edge of the outer ditch to form a sort of glacis. On the south side also, there was a second mud wall on the outer edge of the ditch.

Kot.

The additional protections on the south and east sides of the fort prove that the enemy of the local king was in those directions. And since the citadel or rather the palace, about 300′×450′, occupied the south-east portion of the inner area, that was a reason why the fort walls were made *pucka* with solid brick-work on those sides. This palace had also a ditch to protect it the more. The inner area is higher than the outer. There was a brick bastion on the southern wall of the fort, whence the palace wall starts northward. Three hundred and thirty feet east of the western fort wall, and about 80 feet east of the western palace wall, was a rectangular structure, about 40′×42′, of which the walls can still be traced without excavations. This mound is about 8 feet high, most probably marking the site of an ancient temple, on the east of which was a long tank. In the middle of this tank is a causeway leading southward to a small gate, that gave access to the palace from that side. The main gate on the north communicated with the fort gates on the east and west. There is a small well near the western wall and a few remains, but no indications of any large building in bricks were traced. Although the fort is not covered with jungle, I could not find the ruins of several brick Stupas and heaps of broken sculptures, and a clear spring of water gushing from the ground near a ruined and small Stupa, as mentioned by Dr. Führer, who calls the Kot Kudai. The fields around the fort are all open and cultivated, except the northern tract which is covered with jungle.

Palace.

A temple site.

GUTIVÂ. (See Plate XVII.)

About 4 miles south and a little west of Tilauvâ-Kot, and about 3 miles west and a little south of Taulivâ is Gutivâ. In the centre of the village is a large brick Stupa, 68 feet in diameter, and still about 9 feet in height. Seventy feet south-west from the centre and $32\frac{1}{2}$ feet from the outer rim of the Stupa stands the lower portion of an ancient pillar of the Priyadarsi style, of which the upper portion is gone. Only a small portion is visible above the ground, which is known as *Phutesvara* Mahâdeva, "the broken lord." Major Waddell re-excavated around it down to 10 feet, and the round face of the lower portion of the pillar became visible; for Dr. Führer had opened it before. It stood on a large granite slab, 7′×5—′$8\frac{1}{2}$″×10″ thick. The pillar itself is hard sandstone of a yellowish colour, as is the case with all constructions

Stupa and pillar broken.

See Plate XVI, Fig. 2.

of a similar shape. The pillar stands 1′-10″ and 1′-10½″ from the eastern and southern, 2′-2½″ from the western, and 1′-1½″ from the northern edges of the pedestal. Below the pedestal is brick masonry, as the bedding for the pedestal and pillar. The girth of the pillar is respectively 8′-7″ and 8′-2″ at 1′-10″ and 6′-8″ above the pedestal; 4 feet 6 inches above the pedestal are four rough squares, 6″ in each side, which are a little in relief from the polished surface.

There are three fragments of this pillar lying neglected in the village, of which one is a portion of the bell-shaped base of the capital which crowned it. It is 1′-7″ in height and still about 1′-3½″ broad. It has the usual festoons, broad and narrow, respectively, 2″ and 1¼″ thick, which are, however, defaced. These fragments are called *gutis* (broken pieces), from which the name of Gutivâ is derived. Lori Ahîr of the local legend is said to have played with them by throwing them up and catching them with his hands.

How Gutivâ is derived.

Returning to the Stupa, which I had traced by superficial excavation, Major Waddell dug a deep trench from the centre to the circumference in the direction of the pillar. In the centre, he broadened the hole to 6′-6″ in diameter and 9-3″ in depth. The solid brick-work terminated at 7′-6″ from the top. Going down 1′-9″ further down in the soil, he found a large number of bones, which did not appear to have belonged to man. The teeth were many and certainly belonged to animals. A few pieces of charcoal were also discovered. There was nothing interesting in them. The original central hole, which came down from the top, was about 6″ wide, where, at the time of the construction of the Stupa, a wooden pole, called Linga in Nepâl, was most probably fixed to describe the circumference, as it rose decreasingly and to support the *Torana*, *Chuṛâmani*, and *chhatra* (umbrella).

Bones—not human—found under the Stupa.

On the north of the village is an ancient ditch, and about 200 feet south of the Stupa is an ancient tank. About two furlongs north of Gutivâ is a large mound, on the east and south of which are two tanks. And on the west there appeared the dry bed of an ancient ditch or channel. Excavations might yield some remains.

Lori-Kudân.

About a mile east of the village of Gutivâ and about 1½ mile west of Taulivâ is Lori-Kudân, on the east of which is a row of four ancient mounds, north to south. The northernmost appeared to be a Stupa of solid brick-work, still about 30′ high, of which the superficies was covered with plasters, and concrete as is still visible on the top. On three sides of it bricks have been removed long ago by a *Bábáji*, who erected his huts here. The next mound, just south of it, is the largest and highest of all the four. It had a compound wall on the four sides, which had been removed some years ago. Ascending about 20 feet, I saw another wall, from which bricks are being removed by the villagers. Going up further, a third wall was traceable on the summit about 40′ high from ground level. Here terracotta elephants and horses are dedicated to the spirit of Lori Ahîr, who, the local legend says, was a great giant and used to leap from one mound to the others. On the east of this mound is an ancient tank, full of lotus plants.

Four mounds.
Stupa.

A monastery.

A local legend.

The third mound is a low one, about 250 feet south of the largest one. The walls of a room are traceable here.

The fourth mound appears to be a structure of solid brick-work, on which a modern temple sacred to Siva has been raised by the villagers. On the south of the temple the line of the ancient platform is clearly visible.

These mounds are worth excavation, as being very promising of results; and I have reasons to believe that the largest mound will turn out to be the débris of an important monument, most probably a Buddhistic monastery.

BARDEVÂ.

Bardevâ is a small village, half a mile south-west of Taulivâ. About a furlong south of it, is a small mound of a Mahâdeva temple, close to which are a carved stone and a headless *Nandi*, the sacred bull. The local legend, that I heard from a shepherd boy, is that this *Bard* (bull) used to become a living one during every night and feed upon the standing crops in fields in the neighbourhood to the great loss of the villagers. At last a Thâru, who had less dread of the divine beast than the other low caste Hindus, cut off his head, which was taken to the temple at Taulivâ. From *Bard*, the name Bardevâ is derived.

A stone bull (Bard).

SISANIÂ.

Sisaniâ, distinguished from two others of the same name, as that of the Pâṇṛekî, is situated about 5 miles south and a little east of Taulivâ, and a mile and-a-half north of the 47th pillar, which marks the boundary between the Nepâl and the British territory. It has a large mound, about 700 feet square, in which there were foundations of several brick edifices. From these the village zemindar is removing the bricks, which are very large in size, like those of the Piprâvâ Stupa. On the north and east are two small mounds. On the east of the big mound and south of the smaller and eastern one is the vestige of a ditch; and on the west is a well, from which also the bricks have been removed. On the south is a tank, on the west of which is a village. On the south of the village is another large piece of high ground, where also the ancient town must have extended. On the south of this, again, is an ancient tank, full of lotus plants.

A large mound and vestiges of several edifices.

CHAPTER IV.

RUMMIN-DEI. (See Plates XVIII and XIX.)

General description.

RUMMIN-DEI is about 6 miles north-east of Dulhâ and Boundary pillar No. 35, and about 2 miles north of Bhagwânpur, which is the head-quarters of the Nepâlese Tehsil. About a mile north of Paṛaṛia village, is a very high ground extending east to west for about two furlongs and about a furlong north to south. It represents undoubtedly the site of an ancient town. There are some tanks on the west and south sides.

The main mound.

About 500 feet on the north of this site, and beyond a long tank, now dry, is another rectangular plot of elevated ground, about 300′×400′, which appears to have been once surrounded by a wide ditch, and access to which was had from the south-east. This is the sacred site of Rummin-dei, who is known throughout the Tarâi as a local goddess of some celebrity. The Pâhâries, hill-men, call her Rûpa-dei. She is believed to grant the prayers of her devotees, who bring her offerings of eatables, goats, and fowls, that are sacrificed, and fed here with great ceremony. And hence her popularity has increased amongst the simple folk of the Tarâi.

Modern temple of Rummin-dei. Plate XX, Fig. 1.

This Rummin-dei is represented by a collection of broken sculptures of antiquity, which are kept in the shrine of an ancient temple lately repaired and dwarfed into an ugly shape. This temple occupies the highest plateau of the big mound on the north-west of the elevated area, enclosed by the ditch. About 16′ north of this temple is another of smaller size. About 100′ south of this temple is a small tank whose water is clear and drinkable. On the east of the tank is a small mound, and about 100′ on the north-east of this is another.

Inscribed Pillar, Plate XX, Figs. 2, 3, 4.

About 45′ west of the north-west corner of the temple of Rummin-dei and about 25′ below the top of the mound, rises an inscribed pillar, around which is a sort of brick railing. I cleared round the base within the enclosure down to about $5\frac{1}{2}'$, but could not go down to the foundation. The pillar, of which the lower girth is 7′-9″, is $2'$-$7\frac{1}{4}''$ in diameter. It is in hard sandstone of the usually yellowish colour, and rises to a height of 21′ or so. Its upper portion is gone and of what remains the top is split into two halves,

Capital. Plate XVI, Fig. 3.

the line of fissure coming down to near the middle height. The capital was of the usual bell-shaped form, of which the base, broken into two halves, exists in the compound of the temple. This fact proves that the pillar was complete, when one day a lightning flash penetrated it from above, splitting it into two halves, so far it was then exposed above the mound. The stone horse, which crowned the capital, is gone with the upper portion of the shaft. The capital shows the usual festoons in the face of the big cyma (*Padma*), under which and in the centre is a hole, 5″ in diameter and 1′ in depth, in which was fitted the copper mortice, that was fixed above the shaft.

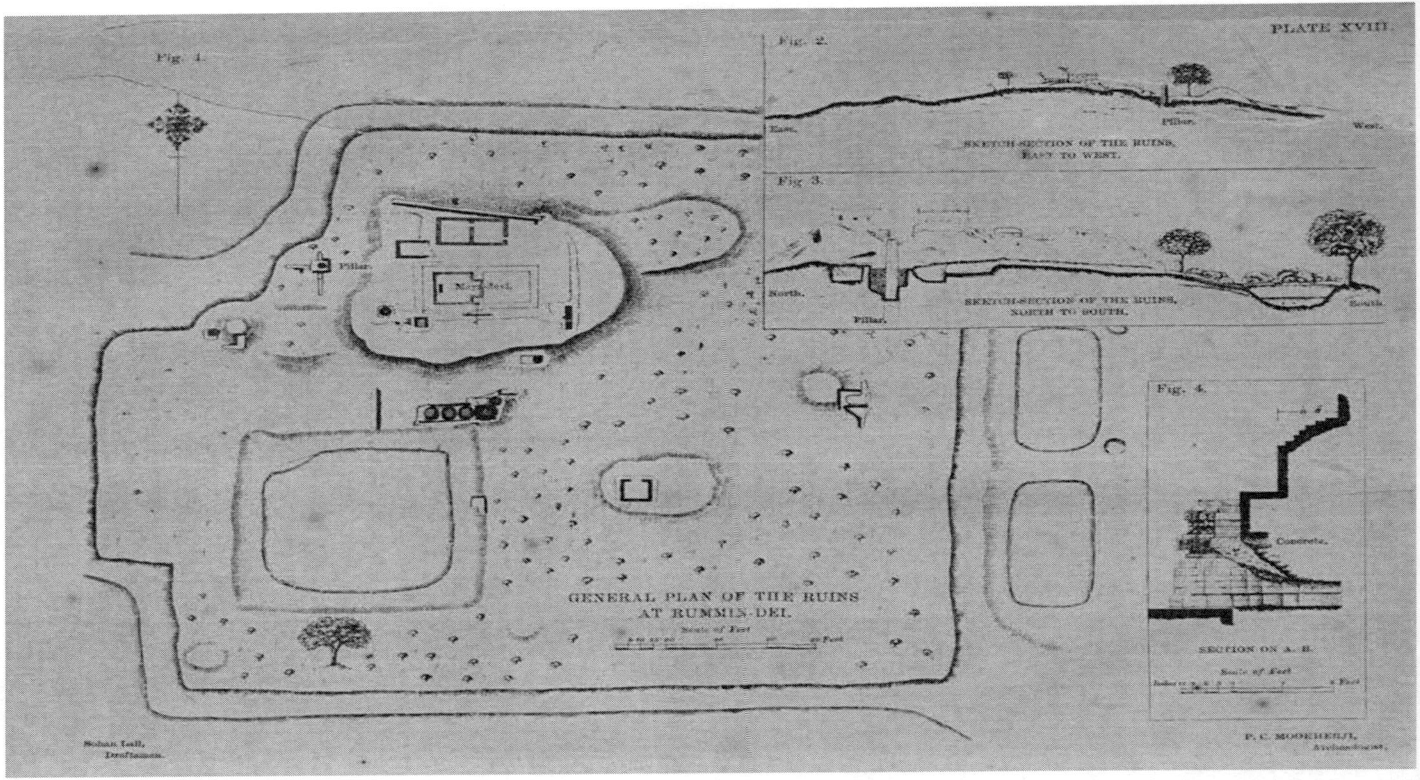
PLATE XVIII.
Fig. 1.
Pillar.
GENERAL PLAN OF THE RUINS
AT RUMMIN-DEI.
Scale of Feet
Fig. 2.
East.
Pillar.
West.
SKETCH-SECTION OF THE RUINS,
EAST TO WEST.
Fig. 3.
North.
Pillar.
South.
SKETCH-SECTION OF THE RUINS,
NORTH TO SOUTH.
Fig. 4.
Concrete.
SECTION ON A. B.
Scale of Feet
Sohan Lall,
Draftsman.
P. C. MOOKERJI,
Archaeologist.

Brick railing.

As regards the enclosure, which is 1′-6″ from the pillar, the walls showed different ages of buildings—the lowest courses exhibiting very large bricks, most ancient in style; and this portion is about 5′-6″ below the top, where the wall has a sort of dentils. The middle wall, above the lowest, is 2′-8″ high and is of subsequent period. The upper wall is of later construction; it shows dentils, about 8″ wide, and each made of two bricks. Above and below the dentils, two lines of bricks recede about an inch, above and below which, again, the courses show rounding off in the upper edges. On the west, the wall rises to a further height of about 3′, where it has fallen. Beyond the enclosure-wall, I excavated on the north, west, and south. The northern trench showed a very thick layer of brick rubbles, and I did not go sufficiently deep to see how the original structure extended on this side. In the western trench a wall 3′-7″ long was exposed, about 4′ from the pillar. And in the southern trench I found, after cutting through a thick layer of rubbles and about 6′ in depth, a brick pavement, which extended in different directions I do not know how far. For, the time being short, and the days becoming hot, I had to stop this, along with other excavations, in order to close my tour.

Further excavations and a brick pavement exposed.

Priyadarsi inscription.
Plate XX, Fig. 4.

On the north-west face of the pillar, and at the level of the upper wall of the enclosure, there is an inscription in the ancient *Pâli*, in five lines, which record that "King Priyadarsi, beloved of the gods, having been anointed 20 years, came himself and worshipped saying 'Here Buddha-Sâkyamuni was born.' And he caused to be made a stone (capital) representing a horse (*Silâ-Vigadabhi; Sanskrit, Vigardhabhi* or *Vikatabhri*;) Dr. Bühler, however, explains it to be as 'a stone slab having a large representation of the sun') and he caused (this) stone pillar (*Silâthabhe=Sanskrit, Stambha*) to be erected. Because here the worshipful one was born, the village of Lumbini-grâma has been made free of taxes and a recipient of wealth." This important inscription sets at rest all doubts in regard to the birth-place of the Buddha; and I have satisfied myself that the *Stambha* stands in its original site, not having been removed from elsewhere. On the northern face of the pillar, and towards the present top, there are several pilgrims' marks, among which the Tibetan formula is inscribed in bold characters. It being translated means "O! the jewel is in the lotus"—the jewel being the god, and the lotus, the human heart, that is, the divine reflection is in man's mind, where alone he is to be worshipped. Fifty feet south-west of the *Stambha* is a mound of rubbles, which, on excavation, on the south and west slopes, showed solid brick-work limited by walls on those sides. One wall coming from the north turns to the east, and from this a cross-wall goes towards the south as shown in the plan. This monument was most probably a Stupa.

A Stupa.
See Plate XVIII, Fig. 1.

On the east of the *Stambha*, the big mound rises considerably, to about 15′, the whole being full of rubbles and bricks. And 45′ east of the pillar is the dilapidated mass of the temple of Rummin-dei. On examining it minutely, I detected a course of the bricks below, on the south side, which I ordered to be cleared. On further excavation downward, two more courses were exposed. Here the concrete pavement of the compound became visible. Just below the walls already exposed, I saw a carved brick, which, on further clearing, was found to be in line with others of similar style. On going

The anterior temple of Mâyâdevi exhumed.
See Plates XX and XXII, Fig. 7.

down further, a very beautiful bay (*Rathaka*) of masonry in carved bricks was exposed. At the two ends of the *Rathaka*, which was the central one, I traced others receding from one another, till the corners were reached. Then I turned towards the west and north sides, where similar arrangements of the ancient walls were brought to light. Now counting the *Rathakas*, and leaving aside the minor projections, I found the number to be seven on each side, which proved that the temple was of that class of plans, known in *Silpasastras* as *Saptaratha*, the seven-bayed one.

Exquisite plinth existing. See Plates XXI and XXII.

Of this very interesting temple, the wall, about 5′ high, only, up to the plinth, remains in a very precarious condition. And that portion is most gracefully composed of carved bricks. The wall in the lowest portion is plain, four bricks high, above which two courses recede by about an inch, which, again, goes back by a bend in the vertical line. Then the neck (*Galá*) appears in a single course in a sort of background, above which is a band of ornaments in two courses of bricks beautifully carved in circular designs. Above this is a floriated cyma, standing on a fillet in a single course. There is another *Galá*, above which is a band, done in *Dásá*, which supports a course decorated with beads. Above this is the big cyma (*Padma*), which occupies the middle of the plinth-wall. This *Padma*, which is rather plain, is relieved in each *Rathaka* with a triangular projection, floriated in graceful designs. The Padma is surmounted by a course of beads, above which is a third *Galá*. Then a band projects about 2 inches, which is carved with wavy floriation and other decorations, and is crowned with a cyma, carved with lotus-petals. Then the fourth *Galá* makes its appearance in a hollow line, above which is an ornamented *Dásá* and a *Kumbha*, the torus of the Greek architecture, done in two courses. Then another cyma is again ornamented with lotus-petals; and the plinth height, 5 feet, is finished up with a course of bricks carved in lines of square and very little holes.

Ante-chamber Vajra Varâhi and other relics. Plate XXIV, Fig. 1, and Plate XXVI, Figs. 1, 2.

Attached to the shrine of Rummin-dei on the east was an ante-chamber, of which the lower walls still exist below the modern ones. Within, I saw several fragments of ancient sculpture. The statue of Vajra-Varâhi, split in two halves across the breast, and 4 feet high by 2 feet 1 inch broad, is all defaced. A group of three standing figures, of which one is a female, being 2′ × 1′ 8″ in size, appears to have originally belonged to the left jamb of the temple door. A third fragment is the head of Pârvati from a group statue of Gauri-Sankara. Besides, there are other figures and heads, more or less broken. There are also bases of pillars, square and circular, with the usual mouldings, fillets, beads, and cyma. But the most interesting is the bell-shaped capital of the Priyadarsi *Stâmbha* and the head of Mâyâdevi, the mother of the Buddha.

Inside shrine.

Entering the shrine by the door, which is on the east side, and going down half-a-dozen steps, the headless group of Mâyâdevi became visible in the rather dark room. It most probably occupies the original position assigned by the architect. On replacing the head, which I brought from outside, the group became quite full of meaning. It is probably of the earliest period of Buddhistic sculpture. Mâyâdevi is represented as holding a branch of the Asok or Sâla tree at the time of her delivery; while her three attendants are helping her in different ways. Below and between them stands the infant Badhisattva. The figures are all defaced.

The floor of the shrine is about 5 feet below the level of the ground or rather summit of the mound on the outside. But allowing 1 foot for the lowest portion of the Mâyâdevi statue, which I think stands *in situ*, and 2 feet for the double pedestal, on which the image stood and about 2 feet for the brick basement, on which the stone pedestal was placed, the original floor must have been below the present one by at least 5 feet. This calculation brings down the original floor to about 20′-9″ (5′+14′-9″+1′) below the present roof, while the lowest course of the plinth wall on the outside is about 16 feet below the same height. It thus makes the inner floor lower by about 5 feet from the outside level of the courtyard. This fact shows that the basement of the original temple exists embedded in the mound considerably down, which judicious excavation will most probably bring to light. It is not possible that Kâlâsoka, who came here with Upagupta as his guide, and might have presumably built the first temple of Mâyâdevi, while raising the pillar with his inscription, did so on a mound. It does not stand to reason that a mound of ruins was formed within one hundred years after the death of the Buddha. The temple of Mâyâdevi, of which the exquisite plinth I exposed some 8 feet below the level of the plateau, must, therefore, have been built subsequent to the decay of the original fane, but long before the visit of the Chinese pilgrims in the 5th and 7th centuries, who saw only one Asoka (Asathva) tree in the sacred place, where Mâyâdevi gave birth to the Bodhisattva.

The original temple of Kâlâsoka suspected to exist below the anterior one.

I may bring to prominent notice the sculptured group of Mâyâdevi. Its size is about 5½′ by 3¼′ in height and breadth. Though it is completely defaced, yet, from what remains, it appears to be once an excellent example of the ancient art, being of that style of workmanship which is generally associated with the time of Asoka the Great. This group-statue is of the yellowish kind of stone, which was employed in the edict pillars and in the two famous Yaksha door-keepers (Dvârapâlas) of Pâtaliputra, now in the Calcutta Museum. The composition of the group is no less spirited than artistic. The group consists of four female figures, of whom that on the right is Mâyâdevi. She stands in a graceful attitude, holding the branch of a Sâla tree with her right hand, while with her left she adjusts her lower garments. The head and body are defaced, but the background above shows delicate gradation of relief in exhibiting the branch and leaves of the tree. The contours of the head and hands show the skill of a master-hand, and her hair falling in wavelets on her left shoulder maintains the balance with the right hand raised up to hold the branch. Dignified action is exhibited in her whole attitude.

The group-statue of Mâyâdevi described. See Plate XXIVa, Fig. 2.

On the right of Mâyâdevi, and immediately below her right hand, stands, close by, a female attendant of younger age and smaller stature, with her right hand raised to help her. Her pose bespeaks considerate action; while the third figure, probably Prâjâpatî-Gautamî, the younger sister of Mâyâdevi, energetically comes in bringing water, presumably from the tank of the Sâkyas, and bends her person to give it to her, thus reminding us of the suddenness of the delivery. But the fourth figure stands as a spectator, talking and meaning business in her own way of aiding the queen. The queen, however, is already free from the pains of delivery; and infant Bodhisattva descending on the earth from her right side, and having taken the first seven steps indicative of the seven-fold initiation before the attainment of Buddha-hood, stands triumphant, knowing full well that this was his last birth, and that henceforth he was free from the miseries of further re-incarnation. It would be well, if the missing fragments that have peeled off are recovered from the ruins and refixed in their proper places to convey the full meaning of this most interesting and, I should say, historical group-statue, which was probably executed under the orders of Asoka[1] in the second century, after the death of the Buddha.

Bâbâji's Math, two Stupas and relics.

About 16 feet north of Mâyâdevi's temple is the *Bâbâji's Math*, which he built some years ago on ancient foundations. This Sannyâsi, who is now dead, cleared portions of the mound and found in the outer room of the *Math* two small Stupas, which he removed. The basement of one Stupa still remains. Inside the inner room, which was double-storeyed, and of which the roof is now fallen, I saw several fragments of ancient sculpture, among which a large head of the Buddha was noticeable. Immediately on the north, I found, on deep excavation, the northern boundary wall, which terminated near the north-east corner of the *Math*, where it turned towards the south, and where another wall appeared going eastward.

Northern boundary wall.

On the back, that is, west of the *Math*, which faced towards the east, I found, on removing a large mass of rubbish, the walls of a square structure, probably the basement of a *Stupa.* And on the south-west of the Mâyâdevi's temple, I discovered another Stupa, small in size, which is much broken, especially on the north-west side. The basement is square, having rectangular projections in the middle of the sides, and rising in regular gradations of courses in rather plain mouldings. Of the round form of the Stupa, the lower portion, so far as remains, shows some mouldings. On the east of it, and south of the temple, are some foundations of basements, on which, no doubt, stood small Stupas. Twenty-three and three-fourth feet south of the wall of the ante-chamber I found, on excavation, a small platform about $8' \times 4\frac{1}{4}'$, on the eastern end of which is a small Stupa, which was much dilapidated.

Small Stupas on the west and south. See Plate XXIII.

Ghât and five Stupas.

Thinking that there must have been some *ghât*, I excavated on the north of the tank, and found a wall going and rising towards the temple; and then digging eastward, I was successful in exposing four diminutive Stupas in a line, and a fifth on the north-east of the fourth. The southern wall of the basement of these Stupas showed batter. And on the north of the fifth Stupa is another wall.

A mound on the east, where walls were partially exposed.

About 75 feet to the south-east of the five Stupas and $101\frac{1}{2}$ feet south-east of the south-east corner of the temple is a low mound, which, on excavation, showed a square structure, on the north wall of which was once an entrance. It was not completely exposed. On the south-east corner of the structure, a mass of solid brick work was brought to light, of which the original purpose I cannot understand until complete clearance is effected.

Another structure on the south-east.

About 110 feet south-east of the Mâyâdevi's temple is another mound, on excavating which, on the east slope, some walls were traced out, going north and east, of which one proceeded south-east; I could not find how far.

[1] That is to say, the earlier Asoka. I believe that there were two Asokas.

It will thus be seen, that this ancient site is full of ruins. Wherever I excavated walls of ancient structures were brought to light. Vestiges of some eight Stupas were already discovered, and basements of some more were traced. Apart from the inscribed pillar, which records the very fact of the Buddha's birth-place here, which is the most important point in topographical archæology, the discovery of a magnificent temple in carved bricks proves how greatly was the art of architecture advanced in ancient times. The group-statue, though much defaced, is not less interesting. Unfortunately the days becoming very hot, and the Nepâlese having left for the hills, I had to stop excavations; more so, as I fell sick.

SAINÂ MAINÂ. (See Plate XXV.)

About 20 or 22 miles,—they say 9 *kos*,—north of Rummin-dei, are extensive ruins of an ancient town, now known as Sainâ Mainâ, which I visited on the evening of the 19th March last. It lies just at the foot of the lower hills of the Himâlayas, and is hidden in the Sâla forest of the Tarâi on the north and west of Karsâ river. Its ancient name was Mainpur Shahar, beyond which nothing is remembered of its history or kings in the local tradition.

Antiquities hidden in the forest.

Crossing the Karsâ, on the south of which and on the east of the village road of Naraina are two mounds, of which one is dedicated to Siva,—and walking northward for more than a mile in the forest, I came to an open place where is a village, Bankatwâ, so called because it was established after cutting the forest. On the north of the village the ground slopes down considerably to low rice-fields, which indicate that some river flowed here in ancient times. Crossing this channel I entered the forest again; and going north-west for a furlong or so I came upon a mound, locally known as *kot.* It appeared to be the débris of a large temple in stone, of which the basement was in brick. I saw several stones cut into temple mouldings. The pedestal, on which the image of the presiding deity stood, is still *in situ*. The basement was excavated in three places by some villagers of old in search of hidden treasure, which, of course, was not found. The holes are about 10 feet deep, showing solid brick-work all through. One peculiar and long slab, 4′-4″ × 2′ × 5½″ with two square holes 7″ × 7¾″, was lying near the northern hole. This mound is still about 15 feet in height.

Débris of a large temple.

Going about a furlong east of this mound, and through the forest, I saw the site of a group of four or five temples, all ruined,—so much so, that even their basements are rather very low. Here are several carved stones, more or less interesting. One is the *Makara* head of a drain-pipe, 8″ high × 8¾″ long, which is carved in the usual style. The second is a lower piece of a small obelisk, of which the four sides show bas-reliefs in niches. The third is an *Amalaka*, (literally, ribbed melon), that surmounted the *Sikhara*—the pyramidal roof,—of a temple. It is 3′-9¾″ in diameter with a central hole, 1′-7″ wide and 10¼″ thick, the semi-circular ribs being on the outer edge—1′-2″ in half girth. The fourth stone is a piece of architrave, 2′-10½″ long × 10″ high, which shows a carving of leaves. The fifth is the left half of the lintel of a temple-door; it is 2′-3″ × 1′ × 8″, showing an ornamented face of the half of the central niche, two *kirtimukhas*, and a scroll on the left.

A group of temples.

On the south of the group of temples is a small square well, 3′-8″×3′-11″, which is known as Râni-kuyiân, the well of the queen. It is built of long blocks of stones, each almost square in section. It is full of clear water, very sweet in taste. This is the only spot where water can be had in this locality.

Râni-well, square.

Penetrating the forest further, for about a furlong on the north-east, I came upon another well, circular and constructed in stone, which is 8′-6″ in inner diameter. I heard of another well, at some distance from it, and on the north-west. On the south-east of the well is another *kot*, the débris of a large temple, where several stones, carved into mouldings, are lying about. The high mound appears to be a solid mass of brick-work, which has been deeply dug into in two or three places by some villagers of old in search of hidden treasures, forgetting that temple sites are the most unlikely places for the safe keeping of wealth. Two pieces of round stones for the *kalasa*, that crowned the temple *sikhara*, and the figure of a beast, very much defaced, are scattered about in the neighbourhood.

Another stone well,—circular, and a second kot.

Proceeding further in the forest, for about two furlongs on the north-east, and crossing a hilly stream, called Baurâhâ, I came upon the first rise of the hill, on the plateau of which is the remains of a temple. This spot is known as Devi's *sthâna*. Here is a figure of the Buddha, seated in the *Bhumi-sparsa* attitude which is 2′-2″ in width and 3′-3″ in height, and of which the upper portion is broken. The *Singhâsana* shows two scrolls of lotus-petals. Close by is a carved slab, 1′-8″×1′-2″, divided into two compartments, of which one shows an ornament in scroll, and the other, the bas-relief of a lion ridden by a man, and standing on an elephant. About 25 feet further north, is a stone pilaster, 1′-1″×5′-4″ high, which contains a Tibetan inscription, which being translated means "O! the jewel is in the lotus."

Devi's sthân and a seated Buddha.

I was only about an hour exploring the forest, just before the setting of the sun, very rapidly walking over the ruins. I could not, therefore, find time to discover other ruins. But that here was a large town was proved by the extensive ruins in stones and bricks being thickly scattered about the place, that I saw on my path.

THE TWO SISANIÂS.

Leaving Rummin-dei on the morning of the 29th March last, I discovered the débris of a temple of Mahâdeva on the north of the village Mânori. It is on the bank of an ancient tank. The temple is of bricks, of which the inner shrine is 6′-9″ × 7′-9″. The *Linga* is 1′-11″ in diameter and 3′-7″ in circumference. This site is worth excavation; for I have reasons to believe that here the remains of ornamented plinth, like that of Mâyâdevi, will most probably be brought to light.

A Mahâdeva temple discovered.

About 4 miles north-west of Rummin-dei is Baṛi Sisaniâ, on the west of the hilly stream of Kothi. On the north of the village is a large mound of ruins, rectangular in plan, where brick walls can be traced. On this is a small shed, in which is collected a number of broken sculpture, worshipped by the villagers as Durgâ. The most interesting is a bust of the goddess, of which the lower portion is gone. On the back of the head is the aureolê, partially

Mounds and broken sculptures known as Durgâ, at Baṛi Sisaniâ.

Plate XXVI, Fig. 8.

broken. The face is rather long. About 50 feet north of the Durgâ mound, is a smaller one known as *kuiyán* (well), whose outer platform is 11′-0″×12′-5″. On the south of the well is a small collection of carved stones, which showed that there was a stone temple here. On the west of the well is a line of brick rubbles, which evidently marks the position of the boundary wall. On the north is the remains of a tank, and about a furlong further north extends a forest along the bank of Kothi and beyond. Half a mile south of the Sisaniâ is the small village of Mahtiniâ, where is a little *Linga* of ancient times, which appeared to have been brought from elsewhere—probably from Rummin-dei itself, for there I heard that a *Linga* and other relics were stolen a few years ago.

Ruins at Chhoti Sisaniâ.

Chhoti Sisaniâ is about a mile west of the Baṛi Sisaniâ. On the north of the village is a circular mound, made up of brick rubbles, which is known as *Sati-sthán*, presumably from the fact of a widow being burnt alive along with her dead husband, long ago. To her a temple was built here, of which the débris now forms the mound. About 50 feet east of it is a spot, held sacred to Barm-deo. But the large mound is about a furlong south-east of the village. It is known as *kot*, being a rectangular ruin, where once stood a brick building of respectable size. But no fragment of ancient sculpture or any other interesting feature of the local ruins were noted. Some bricks were arranged in a sort of daïs in the centre of the *kot*, which represents the seat of the sylvan goddess.

Sijuwâ.

Kot.

Sijuwâ is about five miles south-west of Chhoti Sisaniâ, and about a mile and-a-half south of Abhirâmbazar. It is so called from the local goddess Sijuwâ-Mâyi, who had a *kot* here on the south-west of an ancient tank. The *kot* is a rectangular one, about 150 feet east to west and 100 feet north to south. From the different levels and contours of the mound, I believe that there was a large temple with four smaller ones in the four corners. The *kot* is worth excavation, as promising of results.

Dohni. (See Plate XXVI, Fig. 4.)

Débris of a Mahâdeva temple.

Dohni is midway between Rummin-dei and Piprâvâ. It is a small cluster of villages, of which one called Mahâdeva possesses a large mound. It is about two furlongs on the east of the boundary pillar No. 40. The mound represents the ruins of a large temple once sacred to Mahâdeva, as the name of the local hamlet indicates. Scattered about the mound are several carved stones, of which the door-pieces are very interesting.

Carved door-pieces. See Plate XXVI.

The door-pieces were very elaborately carved. The lintel, of which the left half is gone, had 3 inches, amidst different bands of decorations. The inches contained the three chief gods of the Brahmanical pantheon, the central one, presumably the seated figure of Mahâdeva, indicating the presiding deity of the shrine. The right jamb is still embedded in the mound; but the left jamb shows a pair of husband and wife standing in amatory attitude, above which the vertical lines of ornament are done in the different planes of mouldings. The sill is most interesting of all; the centre is occupied by a thick stem of lotus-plant, from which two stalks branch off in wavy lines, enclosing on two sides two birds seated on full-blown flowers within two scrolls. Beyond are two *Makaras,*—four-footed fish with elephantine head, which, being each ridden by a man, seem to swim on the imagined water most energetically, as shown by the bend of their bodies. The door-step is comparatively plain; only two conches (*Sankhas*) are carved. Taken as a whole, this door-frame is decorated in the usual fashion of such works, not differing much from those I saw elsewhere. I prepared a restored drawing of it by locating the different pieces in their proper places.

On the south-west corner of the big mound is a smaller one, where probably was the open shrine of Nandi, Siva's bull, which is always attached to his temple. About 200 feet west of it is an ancient tank. The big mound of the temple débris is worth excavation, as both the *Linga* and the walls, presumably decorated with mouldings, will be exposed without difficulty.

CHAPTER V.

PIPRÂVÂ. (See Plate XXVII.)

Ancient sites thickly dotting the locality.

THIS group of important ruins is in British territory, near the 44th boundary pillar. It consists of a big Stupa, monastery, and other buildings in the neighbourhood. In the Mouzâh of Aligurh, and near the Sisvâ tank, is a mound of bricks; and on the east of that tank is another. In the village of Ganaria is a brick mound; and about a furlong east of it is a very large elevated spot, on which are several mounds. I have heard of several other ancient sites in the Birdpur and Chândâpâr estates, which I could not find time to see. Only the *Dhih* at Rummin-dei, about 4 miles west of Shohratganj, I saw on my return journey.

Stupa.

Confining my attention to Pipràvâ, I excavated a little here and there, in addition to what Mr. Peppé had done before, to enable me to examine the ruins the better. The Stupa, which is near the road and 19·75 miles north of Uska, is a large one of solid brick-work, the bricks being about 16" × 10½" in size. On inspecting it, in February 1897, Mr. Vincent Smith had discovered it to be a Stupa, and had told Mr. Peppé that relics would be found at about the ground level. That surmise turned out true. In January, the latter gentleman continued the excavations. A trench, about 10' deep, was cut, 63'-6", north to south, and about 9' in breadth, 25' from the northern circumference, and below the trench, an area, 10'×9', was cut through the solid brick-work further down. Ten feet below the then summit of the mound, a broken soapstone (steatite) vase, full of clay, in which were embedded some beads, crystals, gold ornaments, cut-stars, etc., were found.

Circular pipe and caskets.

Below the vase, a circular pipe encircled by bricks, which were moulded or cut into required shape, descended to 2', where the diameter narrowed from 1 foot to 4 inches. After cutting through 18 feet of solid brick-work, set in clay, a large stone-box, 4'-4" × 2'-8¼" × 2'-2¼", came into view. Inside the box, five caskets were discovered; four of these were of soapstone and one of crystal.* The crystal casket, 3½" height and 3¼" in diameter, had a handle, shaped like a fish, and was polished to perfection. These urns contained pieces of bones, gold, beads, two figures in gold leaf, elephant, lions, trident, cross and stars and lotus-flowers; also pearls, pyramids, and drilled beads of various sizes and shapes, cut in white or red cornelian, amethyst, topaz, garnet, coral, crystal and shell. The circular hole went down to the box, where it became rectangular, 21½" each side. The box, caskets, and most of the relics are now in the Calcutta Museum.

* Their size is—
(1) 6" high + 4" diameter.
(2) 7½" „ + 4½" do.
(3) 1¼" „ + 3¾" do.
(4) 5½" „ + 5½" do.

Relics.

See Plate XXIII, Fig. 1, Plate XXVIII, Fig. 2.

Inscription in pre-Asoka Pâli.
Plate XIII, Fig. 2.

But the most important of the finds is a short inscription in one line in ancient *Pâli* characters, which is scratched round the mouth of the smaller urn. The late Dr. Bühler translated the inscription as "This relic shrine (Sarira nidhâna) of divine Budha (is the donation) of the Sâkya Sukriti (renowned) brothers, associated with their sisters, sons, and wives."

Rhys Davids translates it differently as "This shrine for relics of the Buddha, the august one, is that of the Sâkyas, the brethren of the distinguished one, in association with their sisters, and with their children and their wives." One point comes prominently in view from this inscription, which is antecedent to the period of Priyadarsi the Great, that the Sâkyas, to whom the Buddha belonged, must have built the Stupa in their country. Kapilavastu should, therefore, be sought not very far from it.

At the middle height, the circumference of the Stupa was cleared; and the diameter was found to be 63′-6″. On clearing a portion of the top, it was found that the circular mass was built up in concentric layers of bricks. A portion of the western circumference was cleared; and going down 7′, the concrete pavement of the platform for circumambulation, 5′-10″ wide, was brought to view. One foot four inches below it was found the brick-work in a sort of three steps. This original platform appears to have been subsequently added to with extra brick-work to make the Stupa stronger and larger, where another platform with concrete pavement, composed of lime and small pebbles, 4′-7″ wide, was constructed beyond and 1′-4″ below the original concrete. The later platform was only 1 foot thick in brick-work, and edged by a line of standing bricks, that is, bricks-on-edge. Beyond this, again, other brick-works appeared, which show that the Stupa had subsequent additions.

Concrete pavement of the platform for circumambulation.

On the south of the upper circumference, another trench was cut, clearing the step-like brick-work now existing. One foot seven inches below the outer curve, a layer of bricks was found, 6′-3″ wide, about 4 feet below which another, 5′-8″ wide, was cleared. About 2 feet down, the last layer, about 2′ wide, was uncovered down to 2′-3″. Here a projection, 2′-7″ broad, and 4″ deep, was traced; below this, was a layer of bricks projecting 5″ further. Calculating from the outermost circumference, we get an approximate total of $63\frac{1}{2}' + 13\frac{1}{2}' + 13\frac{1}{2}' = 90\frac{1}{2}$ feet as the diameter of the whole Stupa.

Circumference and total diameter of the Stupa.

About 40′ south of the outermost circumference is a wall going east to west, of which about 26′ was traced. Eight feet eight inches south of this is the northern wall of a quadrangular house, 81 feet square, which consisted of rows of small rooms on all sides. The outer wall on the south is 3 feet, and on the other sides 2 feet. The corner rooms are comparatively long, about 18′ × 8′; while the intervening ones are smaller and narrow. One peculiarity was found in the southern wall of the courtyard, where some small brick structures, probably hearths for cooking, as suggested by Mr. V. A. Smith, were found. One of the small rooms in the row had an extra thickness in the northern wall, probably the platform for placing water-vessels.

A house on the south.

About 80 feet on the north of the Stupa are the remains of another quadrangular structure, which, like that described above, was exposed by digging a few feet of the low mound. This edifice appears to have been a *Vihâra*, temple, about 70′ × 78′ in size, of which the portico was on the east, about 30′ long by $11\frac{1}{2}'$ wide. The courtyard is $36\frac{1}{2}'$ east to west by 33′ north to south. The verandah was about $7\frac{1}{2}'$ broad; while the back-rooms, on the north, west, and south, were about 10′ wide. On clearing the north-east room, a floor paved with square bricks was laid open. This layer of paved bricks was removed, to find if any other structure was underneath. But nothing was

A Vihâra on the north.

discovered. Brick-pavements were also traced in the courtyard, and in the other parts of the building. In the centre of the courtyard a small pit was dug, in which walls were found. Additional walls were exposed at short distances between the main walls, of which the purpose I could not understand until more fully cleared.

Sanghârâma on the east.

About 106 feet east of the last structure and 88 feet east of the Stupa, are the remains of a monastery (*Sanghârâma*). It is about 148 feet east to west, by about 135 feet north to south. It is a quadrangle of one row of rooms. The portico was on the west, facing the Stupa and the Vihâra; it was about 20 feet broad in clear space. The outside walls of the main structure are about 6 feet in width; while the inner, about 4 feet. There are 22 rooms on the north, east, and south sides; and on the west, seven rooms were traced. The central room, corresponding to the portico, is comparatively broad, being 16′-10″ in clear space, north to south, of which the back-wall on the east was not exposed. On the existing wall, mud plastering was still visible. Here was found a peculiar framework in iron, rusty with age, which was probably fixed to a window or to the wicket of the main door. It was removed by Mr. Peppé to Birdpur, where it is now kept along with other relics, exhumed at Piprâvâ. The entrance, 7′-7½″ wide, in the main wall, had wooden jambs at the sides, as shown in the two recesses at the flanks still existing. On the south of this entrance, and on the outer face of the wall, is a horizontal piece of wood burnt to black charcoal. This, along with other charcoal found in other parts of the building, proved that it was destroyed by fire.

Its peculiarities.

There was no other entrance from outside. One of the peculiar features here is, that the doors of the inner rooms were placed not in the middle, but at one side. The jambs, 2′-1″ wide, project about 4″ from the main wall, which is 3′-8″ in thickness. This door, about 4′ wide, is 6″ from one side wall, and about 6′ from the other. There was no other door to the rooms, which must have been very badly lighted and ventilated, according to our modern notion of comfort and ventilation. But the monks preferred dark cells, the more lonely and ill-lighted the better for the purpose of meditation.

Crypts having no entrance.

Below the level of the doors, which shows the height of the floor, the wall went down to 8′, where the plinth line in double projections appeared, below which the foundation went down to more than 3′, where earth became visible. Now, this great depth of the wall below the door level proves that there must have been a room down below,—the crypts properly,—where the monks used to sit, each in his cell, cross-legged, for the purpose of contemplation, undisturbed by any noise from outside. Access to these crypts was had probably from a hole in a corner in the floor of the upper rooms. From the existence of cells, I came to know that this monastery was at least two storeys in height, if not three. That is the reason why the débris of this *Sanghârâma* is high,—so much so, that it is widely known as the kot (fort) of Piprâvâ.

In the south-east corner of the kot, and at a distance of about 64 feet outside the monastery, is a well 3′-10″ in inner diameter and 2′ in thickness, beyond which is an outer circular wall, of which the inner and outer diameters are 17′-3″ and 20′-3″, respectively. There are two cross-walls, 4′-5″ long, on the east and south between the two circular ones.

Local tradition has it, that underneath this kot, there is a glass palace, Shish-Mahal, where two golden virgins, *Kánchan Kúmáris*, reside. Occasionally sounds of music are heard as coming from below the *Nágaloka*, the serpent region. The imagination of the local villagers, all Muhammadans here, heighten the hidden treasure as of immense quantity. Fortunate, they add, is the pedestrian who, losing his way in the heat of the midday sun of an auspicious day, and when his superstitious imagination is excited to the superlative degree, suddenly sees, for a moment, the two golden girls walking over the ruins of the *kot*.

Local tradition.

About two furlongs east of the *kot* and near the Sisvâ tank, is a mound, where I partially excavated on the south side and found a brick wall, of the earliest style of construction, stretching east to west. And on the east of the tank, I saw a brick mound (*Dhih*) from a distance, which I could not find time to examine closely.

Other ruins.

On the south of the Stupa and at a distance of about 2 furlongs, is another group of ancient mounds on a large piece of elevated land. The central mound is the largest of all, which Mr. Peppé had excavated in the form of a cross, bringing to light a rectangular structure of no mean dimensions. Its courtyard is 21′×23′-7″ and is paved with bricks. There were corridors (verandahs) on all sides, about 6½′ in width, beyond which were the rooms, each about 10′×8′. The existing walls are between 4′-3″ and 2′-6″ in thickness. The brick pavement was found 5′-2″ below the summit of the mound. Here also this house, of which only the middle of each side was opened, the corners being not touched, had its walls going down more than 10′-6″, of what remains; and no opening was visible for doors, which shows that here was also provided the arrangement for the crypts. If this building was secular, then the underground rooms were intended for the safe keeping of household valuables; if ecclesiastical, then they were cells for the Bhikshukas to meditate.

Another house and other ruins.

About 30 feet south-west of the above mound, is another large one, whose interior is rather hollow. In the centre of the hollow, a pit, about 23′×20′, was dug down to about 7 feet, where portion of an ancient building was exposed. Two rooms, each about 8¼′×9′, with other walls going in different directions, showed that the main structure is still underground. But the most promising feature is the circular mound around the hollow, which, I think, covers the most interesting portion of the ancient monument.

Circular mound with hollow within; a structure exhumed in the centre.

About 30 feet north of this circular mound a portion of another structure has been exposed by just superficially scraping the ground. Rooms, each about 9′-0″×7′-6″, with walls about 2′ thick, show a row going westward, of which about 14′ was exposed. The eastern wall was traced to 15′-9″; but since the northern end was not followed, I could not determine how far it went.

Other ruins.

On the east and south of the central mound are five smaller ones, which were not examined by even superficial excavations. South of these the high ground extends to about 300 feet, where are scattered rubbles and broken bricks of ancient days. In one spot of the south-west corner some traces of walls were very indistinctly seen.

Smaller mounds.

About 300 feet west of the Stupa and beyond the ditch, is another low mound where some rooms were traced by superficially digging the ground. On my first visit here, on the morning of the 25th January last, the Munshi of Mr. Peppé, who was conducting the excavations, was told by me that here a building will be found by only just scraping the surface, pointing out the exact spots where the walls were to be detected. On my second visit, I saw that he followed my instructions, successfully laying bare portions of the eastern part of the ancient structure, which appeared to be a quadrangular one. There were traces of several rooms, of which one appeared to be large, being 16½′×15⅝′. On the west of the northern portion of the eastern wall, and at a distance of about 65′, another wall was traced, going towards east and west. Until some portions more of this ancient monument were cleared, it is difficult to say what it was or what its purpose was.

An edifice exhumed on the west of the Stupa.

Such a large group of ancient mounds of Piprâvâ and its neighbourhood proves that the ancient town here must have been an important one, where the Sâkya Buddhists had a large ecclesiastical establishment. The mention of the Buddha's *Sarîra Nidhâna* (relics of his body), and of the erection of the Stupa by his relatives, most probably refer to the Sâkyas who fled from Kapilavastu after its destruction by Virudhaka of Srâvasti, and settled here. It is a well-known fact that the Sâkyas of Kapilavastu got one-eighth of the relics of the saint at Kusinagara, and erected a Stupa at or near Kapilavastu. But the Chinese pilgrims did not see this Stupa at Kapilavastu, which fact shows that it was not there. It is, therefore, clear that the Stupa was erected by the Sâkyas at the place where they were living at the time. But this spot was not far from the ancient city, as evidenced from the mention of the "Sâkyas of Kapilavastu" in the *Mahâparinirvâna-sutra* and other ancient chronicles. The supposition of a Sâkya colony at the spot, now known as Piprâvâ, explains the large extent of the ruins in this locality. And the identification of the Piprâvâ Stupa with that of the Buddha, raised in B. C. 543, might, therefore, stand good. Asoka the Great is said to have, in about 225 A. B. = 318 B. C., extracted some relics from the Kapilavastu Stupa after dismantling and then rebuilding it, and the breakage of the cover of the large stone box in four pieces, and the covers of the two relic-caskets lying apart from the vessels themselves, betray the fact of an interference with the contents after their original deposit, and of the hurried rebuilding of the hemisphere.

CHAPTER VI.

IDENTIFICATION.

I HAVE already commented on the unsatisfactory nature of previous attempts at the identification of Kapilavastu, and on the inaccuracy of many of Dr. Führer's statements, and need say no more on the subject.

Analysing all the information on the subject of the Sâkya places, so far as available from legendary lore and uncertain literature, from the Chinese, Tibetan, and Ceylonese sources, some facts come into prominent view, which require to be borne in mind while dealing with the subject of identification. The first point, therefore, to be noted is, that the Sâkya brothers, exiled from Sâketa or Potala (Ajodhyâ), the capital of the solar dynasty, went in a northern direction to the primeval sâl forest, where they settled and founded a town, near the hermitage of a Rishi, called Kapila. (2) This spot was near the southern slope of the Himâlaya (how far from the low hills was not stated), where a river by name Bhâgirathi used to flow, and where was a lake (presumably the Sâgar of our day in the Tarai, being a large tank in fact). (3) Contemporaneous with Kapilavastu, another town by name Koli or Devadaha was founded; and between these two flowed a small stream, Rohini or Rohita, from which presumably the present Rohin, several miles east of Rummin-dei, is derived. (4) From the Chinese pilgrims we learn that Kapilavastu was between Srâvasti on one side and Lumbini, Râmagrâma, and Kusinagara on the other. Hiuen Tsiang in the "*Records*" says that about 500 *li* south-east from Srâvasti was Kapilavastu kingdom, about 500 *li* east from which was Râmagrâma. (5) According to Fa Hian, Kapilavastu was one *yojana* west of Kanaka Muni's town. But Hiuen Tsiang, in the *Records* of his Itinerary, notes that Kraku Chandra's town was 50 *li* south of Kapilavastu, and 30 *li* south-west of Kanaka Muni's town. (6) Mr. T. Watters, in his article on *Kapilavastu* in the *Royal Asiatic Society's Journal* for 1898, pages 536-537, gives several bearings in relation to the Sâkya city from the Chinese sources. One statement says that Kapilavastu was three days' journey from Srâvasti. Another important statement is that the road from Kausambi to Sâketa proceeded *viâ* Srâvasti to Setavyam, Kapilavastu and Kusinârâ and Pâvâ to Vaisâli. The life of Chih Meng, a Chinese pilgrim, in about 435 A.D., places Kapilavastu some 260 miles (1,300 *li*) south-west of Kisha (Kailasa ?). (7) The several lives of the Buddha note the distances of the chief towns from Kapilavastu. Anupama, near Râmagrâma, was 12* *yojanas*, Râjgriha, 60,—once walked by Buddha in 60 days, and Vaisâli 51 *yojanas*. But the value of the *yojana*† in these different accounts is uncertain.

General considerations and bearings of Kapilavastu.

(1) It was northward of Saketa and south of Himâlaya, where Bhâgirathi used to flow.

* or 3 according to Asvaghosha.

† Yojana originally meant a day's march for an army. "The old accounts say, it is equal to 40 *li*. According to common reckoning in India, it is 30 *li*; but in the sacred books (*of Buddha*), the *yojana* is only 16 *li*." A *yojana* is equal to eight *krosas*, each *krosa* being the distance that the lowing of a cow can be heard. Beals' *Buddhist Records of the Western World*, Vol. I, p. 70.

If a sketch-map is prepared, showing the Buddhistic places in Madhya-desa or the central country, we can roughly indicate where to look for the Sâkya region. Mr. Vincent A. Smith's discovery of Srâvasti near Nepâlganj, and the find of the Rummin-dei pillar, narrowed the field of exploration between them and closer to the latter, within about a dozen miles.

The general trend of the different bearings and distances.

8. The Kapilavastu region was still further narrowed by Mr. Peppé's discovery of the inscription of the Sâkyas and the Buddha's relatives. The Nigâli pillar of Kanaka Muni, and the Stupa at Gutivâ, which probably indicates the site of Krakuchandra, further defined the limit of the search. Dr. Führer was, I think, correct in his identification of the Stupas commemorating the Massacre of the Sâkyas; and if this be so, the possible limits for the position of Kapilavastu are still further narrowed.

The Inscriptions at Piprâvâ Stupa, Rummini-dei and Nigâli Sâgar, as also the Gutivâ pillar further define the position.

Now, there cannot possibly be any doubt that Rummin-dei, the ancient Lumbini-vana, was the birth-place of the Buddha. Irrespective of the descriptions of the Chinese pilgrims, which tally with the present remains here, the inscription alone proves the fact. That the inscribed pillar stands on its original site, is proved by the very nature of the strata of the ruins. Fifty *li*, or about 10 miles west of Rummin-dei, Kapilavastu should, therefore, be searched for.

In this direction, the Nigâli and Gutivâ pillars define the locality further. Gutivâ is 30 *li*, or about 6 miles south-west of Niglivâ, which is actually the case. Kapilavastu must, therefore, lie some distance north of it. Here I propose to make a small correction in Hiuen Tsiang's distance from 50 to about 20 *li*, one short *yojana* of about 4 miles of Fa Hian. For if the place of Massacre of the Sâkyas was at Sâgarwâ, Kapilavastu must lie a short distance south-east. These calculations lead me to look for Kapilavastu at the *Kot* of Tilaurâ, which gives internal evidence that it was the place sought. The actual distance between the Kot and Araurâ, where most probably was the town of Kanaka Muni, is nearly a short *yojana*, that Fa Hian mentions. But the bearing should be the reverse: that is to say, that Kapilavastu was about a *yojana* west of Konagamana's town,—not east, as Fa Hian says.

All evidence narrowing the field of discovery of Kapilavastu to Tilaurâ-kot,

Before proceeding with the internal evidence, I may observe that Tilaurâ fulfils all the external conditions mentioned in the Buddhistic literature. Kapilavastu was said to have been situated on the side of a lake and to the east of a river (*Royal Asiatic Society's Journal* for 1898, page 540). Just on the west of it flows Bângangâ, the Bhâgirathi of some authorities. Bhâgirathi and Gangâ are convertible terms in the scriptures of both the Brahmanas and the Bauddhas. Tilaurâ is near the Himâlaya, of which the lower range is only about 10 miles on the north. It is on the west (and a little north) of Rummin-dei and at a distance of about 10 to 12 miles,—they say 6 *kos*. Then it is about 4 miles north of Gutivâ, where Krakuchandra's remains are located. The only distance and bearing that remain to be checked are concerning Sara-Kupa, the arrow well, which, according to Hiuen Tsiang, was 30 *li* or about 5 or 6 miles south-east of the Sâkya capital. But according to *Lalita Vistâra*, it was ten *krosas*. The "arrow-well" may, therefore, be looked for either at Panreki Sisaniâ, or Piprâvâ,

which fulfils all external conditions.

See Map. Plate I.

according to the distance, that may be accepted. But Piprâvâ appears to be the more likely site of the two; for Rummin-dei's bearing in relation to it is north-east as recorded by Hiuen Tsiang,—though 80 *li* is perhaps more than the actual distance, which is about 6 Nipâlese *kos*.

Other ancient sites not applicable to the requirements of the Sâkya capital.

Before coming to details, I may see whether there is any other likely site fulfilling the conditions of Kapilavastu. The first prominent site is Piprâvâ, which, with its extensive ruins, must have been an important centre of Sâkya establishment. Here I once thought of locating the Sâkya capital. But there is no river close by, nor do the local bearings and distances tally with those of Kanaka Muni and Krakuchandra, and the Himâlaya is very far. I then devoted a passing thought on Sisaniâ,—about a mile-and-a-half north of the 47th boundary pillar. Here are also rather extensive ruins. But there are no remains of a brick fort; and the place is considerably south of Gutivâ and Nigâli. Besides, there is no internal evidence. Next I turned to the other two Sisaniâs, Chhoti and Bari, to enquire whether they together serve the purpose of identification; for Mr. Vincent Smith had called my attention to Fa Hian's statement, that Kapilavastu was about a *yojana* east of Konagamana's town, which was presumably near the Nigâli Sâgar. But though the rivulet Kothi might serve for Rohini as between Koliya and the Sâkya towns, and Mârthi for Bhâgirathi, which is the stretching of the imaginative identification too far, there are no extensive ruins to represent any of the ancient monuments mentioned by the Chinese pilgrims. I then tried my proposed identification at Sainâ Mainâ, as one Chinese account says, that Kapilavastu was surrounded on all sides by dark purplish rocks (*Royal Asiatic Society's Journal* for 1898, page 540), and as there are several ruins in the forest, and just below the hills. Besides, there is a seated figure of the Buddha and an inscribed slab, showing the Tibetan formula of the Buddhist creed, which probably indicates some sacred spot in association with Sâkya Singha. But all the known bearings and distances are opposed to this hypothesis; nor could I trace the remains of a brick fort or Stupa.

It will thus be seen that no other ancient site has so much claim on the identification of Kapilavastu as Tilaurâ, as being situated in the right position and fulfilling all other conditions. The only other walled town in the region is Araurâ-koṭ, which is in a suitable position; but has not the required remains around it, and is too small.

Detail identifications.

Now, coming down to details, I may quote Hiuen Tsiang's description:—"This country is about 4,000 *li* in circuit. There are some ten desert cities in this country, wholly desolate and ruined. The capital is overthrown and in ruins. Its circuits cannot be accurately measured. The royal precincts, within the city, measure some 14 or 15 *li* round. They are all built of brick. The foundation walls are still strong and high. It has been long deserted. The peopled villages are few and waste. There is no supreme ruler; each of the towns appoints its own ruler" (the *Máhto* or *Chaudhuri* of our day). "The ground is rich and fertile, and is cultivated according to regular season. The climate is uniform, the manners of the people soft and obliging. There are 1,000 or more *Sanghárámas* remaining" (*Records*, Volume II, page 14).

See Plate II.

On glancing over the plan and description of the *koṭ*, it will be found that the above quotation applies to Tilaurâ and its neighbourhood, and nowhere else. Here are jungles, here is a brick fort,—the "royal percincts,"—the citadel of the palace of the king, which also can be easily traced. That the brick wall, which is between 9 and 12 feet broad, was strong and high at the time of Hiuen Tsiang's visit, can be easily understood. One difficulty, however, presents itself, *viz.*, the circuit of the royal precincts was, according to Hiuen Tsiang, 14 or 15 *li* = about 2½ miles round; while on measurements, I found it to be about (1,000+1,000+1,600+1,600)=5,200 feet—only about a mile. But there is no evidence that the pilgrim took measurement; more so, when he says of the town that "its circuit cannot be measured," because it was in ruins and covered with jungles as now. Nor had he the inclination or means to do so. I, therefore, take his statement of 14 or 15 *li* as taken from hearsay, being applicable more to the limit of the outside town than to the citadel itself. And this outside town embraced the present Chitrâ-dei, Râmghât, Sânḍwa, and Tilaurâ, thus giving a circuit of about 2½ miles.

The royal precincts, and high and strong brick-walls.

Hiuen Tsiang further says that "within the royal precincts are some ruined foundation-walls; these are the remains of the proper (or principal) palace of Suddhodana Râjâ; above is built a *Vihára*, in which is a statue of the king. Not far from this is a ruined foundation, which represents the sleeping palace of Mahâmâyâ, the queen. Above this, they have erected a *Vihára*, in which is a figure of the queen." Now, searching for the palace site, which must be prominent, I found that the north-western area of the fort serves such a purpose. On digging on the most promising spot, I came upon the original foundation, about 5 feet below the ground level, which showed neat workmanship in brick masonry. Assuming this to be the remains of the palace, I looked for the *Viháras*, which must have been built on anterior foundations and with the ancient materials. And such mediæval remains also were traced at lesser depths of the soil and around the modern temple of Samai-mâyi. These remains showed masonry of an inferior kind, the bricks being not well set, and carved brick, placed here and there without meaning and design, just as may be imagined from the departure of the royal prosperity and the decay of the art of building.

Palace and Vihâras.

By the side of the queen's apartment was another *Vihára*, where she conceived the Bodhisattva as descending from heaven in the form of a white elephant, which event took place on the 30th night of the month of *Uttaráshárha* according to the *Máhasthavira* school, or a week earlier according to some other authority. On laying bare the foundation walls on the east of the modern fane, I came upon some buildings, of which one was octagonal, and the other square, the western wall of these two continuing southward in a line to enclose other edifices, which I did not find time to open completely. One of these two was most probably the *Vihára* of the spiritual conception.

Conception-Vihâra.

See Plate III, Fig.

To the north-east of the Conception-*Vihára* was a Stupa, where Asita, otherwise known as Kâla-devala, prophesied that the infant Siddhârtha was destined to become a Buddha. About 25 feet north-east of the octagonal structure, I saw a small elevated spot, which I thought to be this site. And excavating it, I traced the foundations of two edifices—one sixteen-sided and the other cruciform in plan. Since the sixteen-sided

Asita-stupa.

Plate III, Fig.

structure, of which every alternative side was in recess, and which had a sort of portico on the north, I at once concluded that this must have been the Stupa of Asita,—more so, as the existing remains showed solid brick-work, the very characteristic of a monumental structure.

The Vihâra of Râhula and his mother.

Here I may point out an evident mistake of the compiler of Hiuen Tsiang's travels. The *Vihâra* of Yasodhara and Râhula could not possibly be by the side of the *Stupa* and the elephant-ditch, which were beyond the southern gate of the city or rather citadel. The sleeping apartment of the Bodhisattva's wife must have been situated near the palace of her father-in-law,—in the courts of the queens and princesses. If my surmise is correct, I do not feel any difficulty in locating Yasodharâ's quarters on the north-west of the central tank, being near the south gate of the king's palace. I excavated here and found buildings.

School-house.

" By the side of the queen's (Mâyâdevi's) chamber is a *Vihâra* with a figure of a pupil receiving his lessons; this indicates the old foundation of the school-house of the royal prince." Since this school, where Visvâmitra taught Siddhârtha, might have most probably been situated between the queen's apartments and those of the males', being nearer to the latter, the requirements of this identification will be best met by locating the school on the north-east of the central tank, where on superficial excavation, I partially traced a building.

Sanghârâma.

" By the side of the royal precincts there is still a *Sanghârâma* with about 30 followers in it, who study the Little Vehicle of the *Sammatiya* school." Since by the " royal precincts" I understand the walls of the citadel, I searched for the remains of a quadrangular structure, and I found one just in front of the eastern gate, the only habitable quarter at the time of Hiuen Tsiang's visit, the rest being overgrown with jungles. I excavated here and brought to light the foundation-walls of a rather large building. Its original wall is traceable in the south-west corner; but on the north side, some of the walls appeared to be subsequently added inartistically and irregularly.

Two Deva-temples.

" There are a couple of Deva temples, in which various sectaries worship." Though there were undoubtedly fanes within the citadel, to which the broken sculptures, now worshipped as Devi or Samai-mâyi, must have belonged, the chief ecclesiastical buildings were on the other side of the river Bân-Gangâ, and at Chitrâ-dei, where I brought to light the remains of a very large and magnificent temple. I traced the foundation-walls of other but smaller temples. Chitrâdevi was the name of one of the goddesses still worshipped by the villagers with terra-cotta elephants on the mound of a smaller temple.

Hastigarta.

In front of the south gate was a Stupa, where Siddhârtha threw away a dead elephant, which his cousin, Devadatta, had killed and which caused a deep ditch, whence known as the " *Hastigarta*," the elephant-ditch. About 500 feet south of the south gate of the citadel is a small mound of earth which might represent the elephant-throwing Stupa. And about 100 feet east of it is the remains of a ditch, which becomes a stream during the rainy season ,and which was very likely the *Hastigarta* of the Buddhistic tradition.

"At the south-east angle of the city a *Vihâra*, in which is the figure of the royal prince riding a white and high-prancing horse; this was where he left the city." (*Records*, Volume II, page 18.) But according to *Lalita-Vistâra*, Bodhisattva effected *Mahâ-abhiniskramana*—the great Renouncement—through the Mangaladwâra, the auspicious gate, and left the city, facing the east. And since he rode evidently in an eastern direction, the gate must have been the eastern one. So the *Vihâra* requires to be sought for in front of the eastern gate. Now about 650 feet south-east of the gate is a large Stupa, which I propose to identify with the Stupa of Kantaka's *Nibarttana* (Return), as mentioned in *Lalita Vistâra*. The *Vihâra* of the great Renouncement must, therefore, be sought for somewhere here or nearer the gate, in front of which I have located the *Sanghârâma*. There is no indication of a building beyond the south-east gate. But if the gate is taken to be that of the city wall, then this spot might be sought for at Sândwâ, where, however, I could not find sufficient time to search minutely.

Vihâra of Mahâ-abhiniskramana.

"Outside each of the four gates of the city, there is a *Vihâra*, in which there are respectively figures of an old man, a diseased man, a dead man, and a *Samana*," at the sight of which he got disgusted at the world and its pleasures. Fa Hian mentions only one Stupa, where he turned his carriage round on seeing the sick man after he had gone out of the city, by the eastern gate—(Legge's *Fa Hian*, page 65.) There is a mound in front of the north gate, which is north-east of Asita's Stupa. In front of the east gate, there is an ample elevated ground to accommodate a *Vihâra* beside the *Sanghârâma*. On the south, there are two Stupa-like mounds at Derwâ, where might have stood another *Vihâra*. But on the west, there is a semi-circular mound within which and the inner ditch, I found, on excavation, a large room, which most probably represents a *Vihâra*,—for a building just on the outside of the citadel wall could not serve any other purpose. But if the western gate be assumed as existing west of Chitrâ-dei, then the *Vihâra* should be sought for beyond the ditch, which want of time did not allow me to do. The town of Kapilavastu beyond the citadel was, at best, a cluster of villages with open fields here and there, as we still see in modern cities. So it is difficult to make anything out of Hiuen Tsiang's account, which is here very meagre in some points.

The Vihâras of four signs.

"To the south of the city, 3 or 4 *li*, is a grove of Nigrodha trees, in which is a Stupa, built by Asoka-Râjâh." (*Records*, Volume II, page 21.) Three or four *li* is less than a mile. I could not find any Stupa about that distance, south of the koṭ of Tilaurâ. But about 2 miles further south are the ruins of Lori-Kudân, where is a solid brick mound, very like a Stupa, on the south of which is a large structure, still about 40 feet high. This structure might represent the famous Nigrodha monastery, where Suddhodana received his son as the Buddha, and which he dedicated to his church.

Nigrodha-Arâma.

"By the side of the *Sanghârâma* and not far from it, is a Stupa" where "Tathâgata sat beneath a great tree with his face to the east and received from his aunt (step-mother Prajâpati Gautami) a golden-tissued *Kashâya* garment. A little further on is another Stupa where Tathâgata converted eight kings' sons and 500 Sâkyas." (*Records*, Volume II, page 22.) If the *Sanghârâma* is understood to be that of the Nigrodha, there is no

Kashâya-stupa.

difficulty in identifying these two Stupas with the two other mounds of Lori-Kudân, on the southernmost of which stands the modern temple of Siva. But if the *Sanghârâm* is taken to be that "by the side of the royal precincts," then there might have been two small *Stupas* of the diminutive form I exposed at Rummin-dei, in the neighbourhood, which might have altogether disappeared. It is, however, not reasonable to think, that Hiuen Tsiang once mentioning a monument goes off to describe several others and then returns to the first to note others in its immediate neighbourhood, a confusion, not naturally fallen into.

Stupa of athletic sports.

"Within the eastern gate of the city, on the left of the road, is a Stupa ... where the prince Siddhârtha practised (athletic sports and competitive) arts." If the gate refers to the citadel, there is ample, though low, space on the south of the ancient road from the eastern to the western gates, which might have served the purpose of recreation ground.* But if it refers to the town-wall somewhere near the village of Baṛi Tilaurâ, I have not found any mound of bricks, which would represent the Stupa.

Isvara-deva.

"Outside the gate ('eastern'?) is the temple of Isvara-deva. In the temple is a figure of the Deva made of stone, which has the appearance of rising in a bent possition." (*Records*, Volume II, page 23.) The site of such a temple was not found either on the east of the citadel gate or in the neighbourhood of Tilaurâ. But if the fate is understood to be that of the south wall of the town, then no difficulty is felt in identifying the Isvara as that of *Taulivá-isvara*, the well-known *Linga* of Mahâdeva, to worship which people congregate from great distances. The present temple stands on a high brick mound. There are other ruins in the neighbourhood.

Stupa of tournament.

"Outside the south gate of the city, on the left of the road, is a Stupa ; it was here the royal prince contended with the Sâkyas in athletic sports (arts) and pierced with his arrows the iron tragets." Here I have strong reasons to believe that the south gate belongs to the citadel, and not to the city. I have elsewhere observed that the ancient town of Kapilavastu consisted of a cluster of villages with extensive fields between them and round the citadel. There was, therefore, no occasion of going out of the town, especially when it is recorded in the *Lalita-Vistára*, that Gopâ or Yosadharâ, the bride-elect, planted the flag of victory in the arena in the court of the palace. It is against custom and social etiquette that the daughter-in-law of a Râjâh went outside the town for the purpose. I suspect that Hiuen Tsiang made a great confusion between the citadel and the city; where he mentioned the latter we should understand the former. If my surmise is correct, then one of the two Stupa-like mounds at Derwâ, about a furlong south of the citadel, might turn out to be the very one I am in search of. Beside those mentioned by Hiuen Tsiang, there are others, noted by Fa Hian, such as the Stupa, where the 500 Sâkyas worshipped Upâli, and where the Buddha preached to the Devas, which were evidently outside the town, and of which no distances or bearings are given.

Massacre of the Sâkyas.

"To the north-west of these are several hundreds and thousands of Stupas, indicating the spot where the Sâkyas were slaughtered by Virudhaka râjâ. (Fa Hian mentions only one Stupa.) To the south-west of the place of massacre are four little Stupas . . .

* *Lalita-Vistára* describes the arena of the tournament in the courtyard.

where the four Sâkyas withstood an army." Dr. Führer identified this place of massacre in the forest of Sâgarwâ on the west and south of the large tank called Sâgar, where he excavated extensively. Though hundreds and thousands were not yet found, seventeen were counted in the two excavated spots, and forty-nine subdivisions were cleared in the largest of the Stupas, attached to a monument in a cruciform plan, miscalled a *Vihâra*. But the four small Stupas, south-west of the place of massacre, have not been detected. Most probably there are other Stupas, still buried underground. Sâgarwâ is about 2 miles north of Tilaurâ-koṭ; and it is almost due north. But the bearing, according to both Fa Hian and Hiuen Tsiang, is north-west, which may be explained on the assumption that they might have visited the place by going round from the east to avoid the dense jungle, just as we do now.

Ploughing Stupa.

"To the north-east of the city about 40 *li* (several *li*, according to Fa Hian) is a Stupa, where the prince sat in the shade of a tree (Jambu) to watch the ploughing festival." Six and a half miles north-east of the *kot* lead us to the neighbourhood of Jâdi, where the Jâmuar (presumably derived from Jambu—Jambuar,—which tree abounds its banks) flows. But I did not hear of a mound in the neighbourhood, nor could I find time to explore here. I strongly suspect that many of the monuments, mentioned by Hiuen Tsiang, were not built of bricks or stones, but were mere mounds done up with earth, which might have been washed or cut away by the villagers during the course of ages. That might be the reason why they cannot now be distinctly traced out.

Krakuchandra's Stupas and Pillar, erected by Asoka.

"To the south of the city, going 50 *li* or so, we come to an old town, where there is a Stupa, where Krakuchandra Buddha was born, during the Bhadra-kalpa, when men lived to 60,000 years. To the south of the city, not far, is a Stupa where, having arrived at complete enlightenment, he met his father. To the south of the city is a Stupa, where are that Tathâgata's relics (of his bequeathed body); before it is erected a stone pillar, about 30 feet high, on the top of which is carved a lion. By its side is a record relating to the circumstances of his *Nirvâna*. It was erected by Asoka Râjâ."

If I am justified in reducing the distance from 50 to about 20 *li*, or about 4 miles, the *yojana* of Fa Hian, then the ruins at Gutivâ answer well our purpose of identification; for here is a brick Stupa, near which is the lower portion of an Asoka-pillar, known as Phuteswar Mahâdeva. Since the upper portion is broken, the inscription is lost. This pillar might attest the *Nirvâna* Stupa of Krakuchandra, which I traced, and Major Waddell dug and found a large number of bones, consisting of teeth, thigh bones, etc. They appeared as belonging more to beasts than to men; and it seems very probable that, when long after the death of the saint, the Buddha-lore degenerated into legends, and fables grew into myths, some Bhikshus, long before the visit of the Chinese pilgrims, committed, as they say, 'pious frauds' by burying some bones of cattle and extolling them as the *sariras* of Krakuchandra, and built a Stupa over them.

North-west of this Stupa, I could not find another. But about two furlongs north-east of the village is a very large mound, which might represent either the Stupa of Krakuchandra's meeting with his father, or the place where he was born. But the latter appears to be the more probable site. There are a few ancient tanks in the neighbourhood.

Kanaka-muni's Stupas and Pillar, raised by Asoka.

About 30 *li* or 6 miles north-east of Krakuchandra's town was another, where, in the Bhadra-Kalpa, when men lived 20,000 years, Kanaka-muni Buddha was born, the spot being marked by a Stupa. To the north-east of the town, and not far, is another Stupa, where having attained Buddha-hood, he met his father, and further north is a third, which contained the relics of his body and in front of which was a stone pillar with a lion on the top, and 20 feet high. The pillar, which was raised by Asoka, had an inscription recording Kanaka-muni's Nirvâna. The inscription on the pillar, called Nigâli, near Niglivâ, records that the Stupa of Kanaka-muni was worshipped by King Priyadarsi, when he came here in the 21st year of his reign. Since it is not possible that such a big pillar, about 3 feet in diameter and about 50 feet in length, could have been removed far away from its original site, where it was erected by Priyadarsi, I have reasons to believe that the town of Kanaka-muni might have been very close here. But no brick Stupa was found here, though I searched in the neighbourhood. Most probably there were earthen Stupas like those at Lowriyâ in Bettia; they might have been either washed away, or the earth removed by the villagers for raising their huts; or may be, the bricks might have been removed from the Stupas for the rebuilding of the Aṛâuṛâ-kot, which, I think, represents the town of the Muni. The village about half a mile south of the Nigâli Sâgar is called Thâmuâ, presumably from *Sthambha*-pillar, that of Kanaka-muni, from which the name is derived. On the south of this village, which stands on ancient mounds, is an ancient tank; and on the west of the Nigâli are three or four; which show that, besides the *kot*, there were here extensive inhabited quarters, another large village of an ancient time. Now if this is taken as the town, the bearing of the pillar is north-east, exactly as was mentioned by the Chinese traveller. But if Aṛauṛâ-kot is understood to be the town of Kanaka-muni, the bearing is north-west. I have reasons to believe that the Nigâli Sâgar was repaired and dug again after the visit of the Chinese pilgrims, the excavated earth being thrown over the ruined Stupas, which might have stood here.

Sara-kupa.

Thirty *li* south-east of Kapilavastu—(10 *krosa* according to *Lalita-Vistâra*)—was a small Stupa, near which was a "fountain, the waters of which are as clear as a mirror," which, according to a common tradition, was caused by the arrow of Siddhârtha, while contending with the Sâkya princes in the athletic sports, whence it was known as the arrow-well. "Persons who are sick, are mostly restored to health by drinking the water of this spring; and so people coming from a distance taking back with them some of the mud (*moist earth*) of the place and applying it to the part where they suffer pain, mostly recover from their ailments." Fa Hian says that Bodhisattva "shot an arrow to the south-east and it went a distance of 30 *li*, then entering the ground and making a spring to come forth, which men subsequently fashioned into a well, from which travellers might drink." (Legge's *Fa Hian*, page 65.) Thirty *li* or about 5 to 6 miles south-east of Tilaurâ is Sisaniâ, where are extensive mounds of ancient ruins. On the north-east of the large mound and near the ditch, is a small one which may represent a small Stupa. But if 10 *kos* is accepted as the more correct distance, then the *Sara-kupa* may be looked for at Piprâvâ, from which the bearing to Rummin-dei is north-east, as Hiuen Tsiang records. Not so is the bearing from Sisaniâ, which is due west of Rummin-dei; and the distance is about 12 miles. But the distance between Piprâvâ and Rummin-dei is only 12 miles or so, not more than that. Probably Hiuen Tsiang might have walked in a circuitous way to avoid the forests and wild beasts; and so he recorded the longer distance and the bearing that he found in the last part of his journey. Sisaniâ may, therefore, be the more probable site for the Arrow-well.

LUMBINI-VANA.

Lumbini, according to Fa Hian, was 50 *li* east of Kapilavastu, and according to Hiuen Tsiang, 80 or 90 *li* north-east of the arrow-well, which was 30 *li* south-east of the Sâkya capital. But irrespective of these bearings and distances, Lumbini has been identified with Rummin-dei beyond the possibility of a doubt. The first evidence is the inscription, twice recording the fact of the Buddha Sâkya Singha being born here (*Epigraphia Indica*, Volume V, Part I, page 4.) (2) The pillar stands *in situ*;—there is no indication that it was brought from elsewhere. (3) The high mound is made up of strata of débris, one above another, which proves its great antiquity. (4) The Tilâr Nadi, which Hiuen Tsiang translated as the "river of oil" still exists about a furlong east of the mound, tallying with the bearing and distance recorded by the pilgrim. The number of Stupas and the group-statue of Mâyâdevi, the former of which I discovered during the late excavations, is an additional proof. And the last, but not the least, is the word *Rummindei* itself, which clearly preserves the ancient word *Lumbini*.

Lumbini is undoubtedly Rummin-dei.

The tank of the Sâkyas.

"Here is the bathing tank of the Sâkyas, the water of which is bright and clear as a mirror, and the surface covered with a mixture of flowers. To the north of this, 24 or 25 paces, there is an Asoka flower-tree; which is now decayed, where Bodhisattva was born on the 8th day of the 2nd-half of the month called *Vaisâkha*." The tank, on the south of the mound, exactly tallies with the description given above, and just about 25 paces on the north is the temple of Mâyâdevi, who occupies the shrine in the centre. I carefully exposed the very interesting remains of the temple. It seems that at the time of Hiuen Tsiang's visit this temple was in complete ruins, over which an "Asoka flower" tree (Asathva or Pipal?) grew and then decayed.

Buddha's birth-place.

On the east of this spot was a *Stupa* built by Asoka Râjâ on the spot, where the two Nâgas bathed the body of the prince. About 100 feet east of the central mound is a smaller one, where I partially excavated on its eastern slope. Though the solid brick-work of the Stupa was not touched, some walls were exhumed. If no small Stupa, like those I discovered on the south, is embedded on the eastern portion of the big mound, then this one, most probably, represents the Asoka Stupa. I once thought of the small Stupa, about 25 feet north of the ante-chamber; but since the name of Asoka means some big monument, I gave it up. The big Stupa, 50 feet south-west of the pillar, which I excavated on the south and western slopes, might very well represent the Stupa of Asoka, if there is a mistake in the bearing. To the east of this Stupa were two "fountains" (Legge says "a well"), by the side of which were two Stupas indicating the spots, where the two Nâgas (dragons) appeared from the earth. By the fountain, I understand small tanks; and two small tanks are there on the east, forming a sort of ditch in that direction. On their eastern banks are two small mounds, of which one has been dug out of its bricks,—leaving a smaller circular hole. These two might

Asoka Stupa.

most probably represent the two Stupas where the Nâgas were said to have appeared.

"To the south of this is a Stupas where Sakra, the lord of the Devas, received Bodhisattva in his arms." Since I could not trace any mound on the south and east of the two tanks and the two Stupas, I had to come on the south-west and on the north-east bank of the tank, where I excavated and exposed five small Stupas. Of these, that on the north-east I assign to Sakra.

Sakra-stupa.

"Close to this there are four Stupas to denote the place where the four heavenly kings received the Bodhisattva in their arms." If my identification of the Sakra Stupa stand good, then there is no difficulty in assigning the four Stupas, just on the south-west of it and in a line with one another, to the four Devarâjâs. On the south and west of the Mâyâdevi's temple are some other Stupas, which are close to the pillar. They might represent the four Stupas.

Four Stupas of the four Devas.

"By the side of these Stupas and not far from them is a great stone pillar, on the top of which is the figure of a horse, which was built by Asoka Râjâ. Afterwards, by the contrivance of a wicked dragon, it was broken off in the middle and fell to the ground. By the side of it is a little river, which flows to the south-east. This is the stream which the Devas caused to appear as a pure and glistening pool for the queen, when she had brought forth her child to wash and purify herself in. Now it is changed and become a river, the stream of which is still unctuous." (*Records*, Volume II, page 25.) The pillar is about 45 feet west of the back-wall of Mâyâdevi's temple and, as noted by Hiuen Tsiang, it is split in the middle, no doubt caused by lightning. The bell-shaped capital is also split in two halves, which, no doubt, fell along with the horse which crowned it when the pillar was struck by lightning. As to the "River of oil," there is a small stream about a furlong and half east of the mound still called Tilâr, which is, in meaning, the original of the Chinese translation. But since the Chinese pilgrim mentions it "as a pure and glistening pool" and in the immediate neighbourhood of the pillar, there are vestiges of tanks, on the west, which stretch a long way. Tilâr might have flowed here at the time of Hiuen Tsiang's visit.

Asoka-pillar.

River of Oil.

The inscription of Priyadarsi in the pillar records the name of a village as Lumbini-grâma. A few hundred feet south of the mounds of Rummin-dei is a large elevated plot of ground, where are indications of ruins. This might most probably represent Lumbini-grâma, of which the taxes were remitted by king Priyadarsi.

Lumbini-grâma.

At the time of the birth of the Buddha in 623 B. C., Lumbini-vana was between Kapilavastu and the town of the Koliyas, called Devadâha or Koli. I searched the tract of the country for about 4 miles eastward up to the river Dano, and discovered the name of a small rivulet on the north of the village of Bâghia,* which is still called Kolihâ or Koilihâ. This Kolihâ might most probably represent the town and tribe of the Kolyans.

We have no indications of the several other places and monuments at and about Kapilavastu; of which stray mentions are scattered in the Buddhistic literature of the different countries. But if the Tarâi is minutely explored, I doubt not that several sites of antiquarian remains will be brought to light.

* Bagh'a might be a reminiscence of Vryaghrapura, another name of Devâdaha or Koli.

CHAPTER VII.

RECOMMENDATIONS FOR FURTHER EXPLORATIONS IN THE TARAI,—AND CONCLUSIONS.

AS observed at the end of the third chapter, the survey of the antiquities in the Tarâi has not yet been exhausted. The region of Kapilavastu should be more definitely examined, mapped out, and explored. In the Buddhistic period, there was a sort of highway between Srâvasti, Kapilavastu, Anupiya, Râmagrâma, Kusinagara, and Viasâlî, and another between Râjgriha, Benares, Sâketa, (Ajodhyâ) and Srâvasti, which need to be definitely plotted in a map.

Works remain still to be done.

Irrespective of the details and minor lacunæ, which are to be filled up in connection with the identification of Kapilavastu, there is much work still remaining to be done in the line of excavation itself. The mounds at Chitrâ-dei, Tilaurâ-kot, Rummin-dei, and Piprâvâ-kot, have only been partially excavated. Nothing has yet been done at Lorî-kudân, Araurâ-kot, Sainâ-Mainâ, Dohni, Sohangarh, Chângât, Deve-kî-sthân, and the three Sisaniâs. Full advantage should therefore be taken of the liberal grants of the Nepâl Darbâr, who are willing to help in every way in the work of archæological exploration and survey.

I may therefore suggest that after a visit to Sahet Mahet, exploration may be undertaken near Nepâlganj, a few miles north of which Mr. Vincent Smith believes that he has discovered the ancient site of Srâvasti. The Asoka-pillar, which is said to exist somewhere near Bairât, a deserted site in Parganâ Kolhivâ of Tehsil Nepâlganj, or near Matiâri on the Rapti, and in the same Tehsil, should be searched for.

Programme of next season's tour.

Sahet Mahet and Nepâlganj to be explored.

Since the mounds at Lorî-kudân appear to be very promising, they might be opened at an early date; and the excavations at Chitrâ-dei and Tilaurâ might be carried further.

Mound at Lorî-kudân to be excavated.

It will be worth while to superficially excavate at Araurâ-kot, and the three Sisaniâs, and just to feel what the buried monuments may be.

Araurâ-kot.

Rummin-dei, where we explore on surer grounds, might be surveyed and excavated further; and another visit paid to Sainâ-Mainâ.

Rummin-dei and Sainâ-Mainâ.

The investigation might be followed up in the Eastern Tarâi, an effort being made especially to fix the site of Râmagrâma, which is probably north of the Gorakhpur District. An Asoka-pillar is reported to exist north of Nichhawal. I have heard reports of the existence of other pillars at Barevâ and Maurangarh, north of the Champâran District. The opportunity might be taken to examine the sacred places at Tribeni ghât, Bâwangarh and other sites.

Eastern Tarâi.

The end of the season might be devoted to the search for Kusinagara at Deo Darpâ, some 30 miles north-west of Bhiknâ Thori, where Mr. V. A. Smith suspects it to be and at other likely sites, if my identification of the Pari-nirvâna spot at Lowriyâ does not hold good. The tour might be completed by the end of March or the beginning of April next.

Deo Darpâ.

In concluding my Report, I may give a summary of the results of my work in the Nepâl Tarâi. The first and most important is of course the discovery of Kapilavastu, the position of which I claim to have more definitely determined than Dr. Führer did. The next is the probable detailed identification of several monuments mentioned by the Chinese pilgrims. The third is the identification of some of the monuments at Rummin-dei. And the fourth is the recording of several ancient sites, not known before, all being plotted in a rough map, serviceable for ordinary purposes.

Summary of results attained in last tour.

The time at my disposal did not permit of excavation on any considerable scale except at Tilaurâ-koṭ, Chitrâ-dei, and Rummin-dei. At all of these places, results of interest were obtained. Though my excavations were not rewarded with any inscriptions or important sculptures, the architectural finds were of a very interesting class. Even the Chinese pilgrims did not know that a magnificent temple was erected on the sacred site of the Buddha's birth. The group-statue of Mâyâdevi, though defaced, is unique and interesting, being of the earliest style of Buddhistic sculpture. The discovery of the statue of the Buddha, both in stone and terra-cotta, showed that the art of sculpture was known here long before the *Gupta* period. The magnificent temples that I exposed at Chitrâ-dei and Rummin-dei prominently bring to view the artistic excellence of the Sâkyas; and the forms of the monuments themselves, irrespective of the ornate details, show some very interesting features in the ancient architecture of the Tarâi. The Chitrâ-dei temple is cruciform in plan, relieved with minor projections. The Stupas at Ṭilaurâ-koṭ were octagonal and sixteen-sided in plan, the diagonal or alternate sides being highly recessed,—a feature I have not seen elsewhere in India. These are the chief results I have been able to achieve during the short time allowed me for the purpose.

P. C. MUKHERJI.

PLATE III.

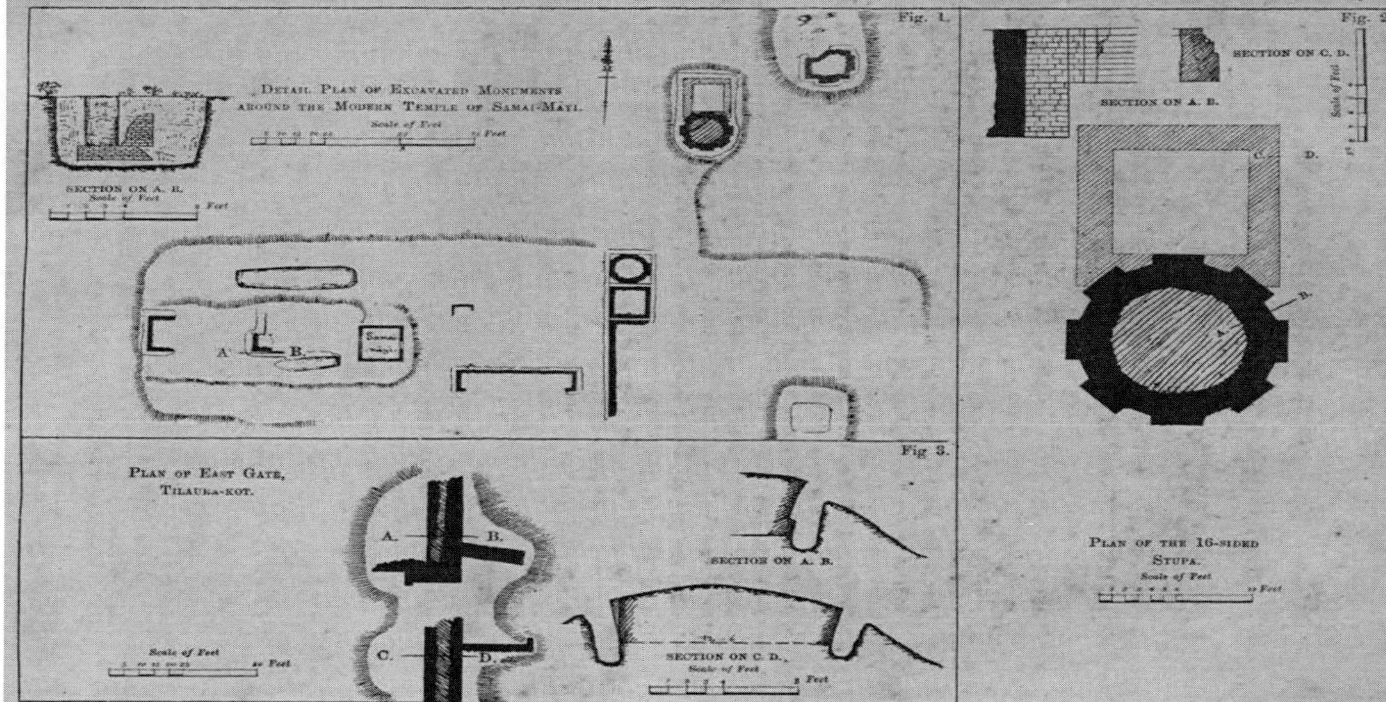

P. C. MOOKHERJI,
Archaeologist.

PLATE IV.

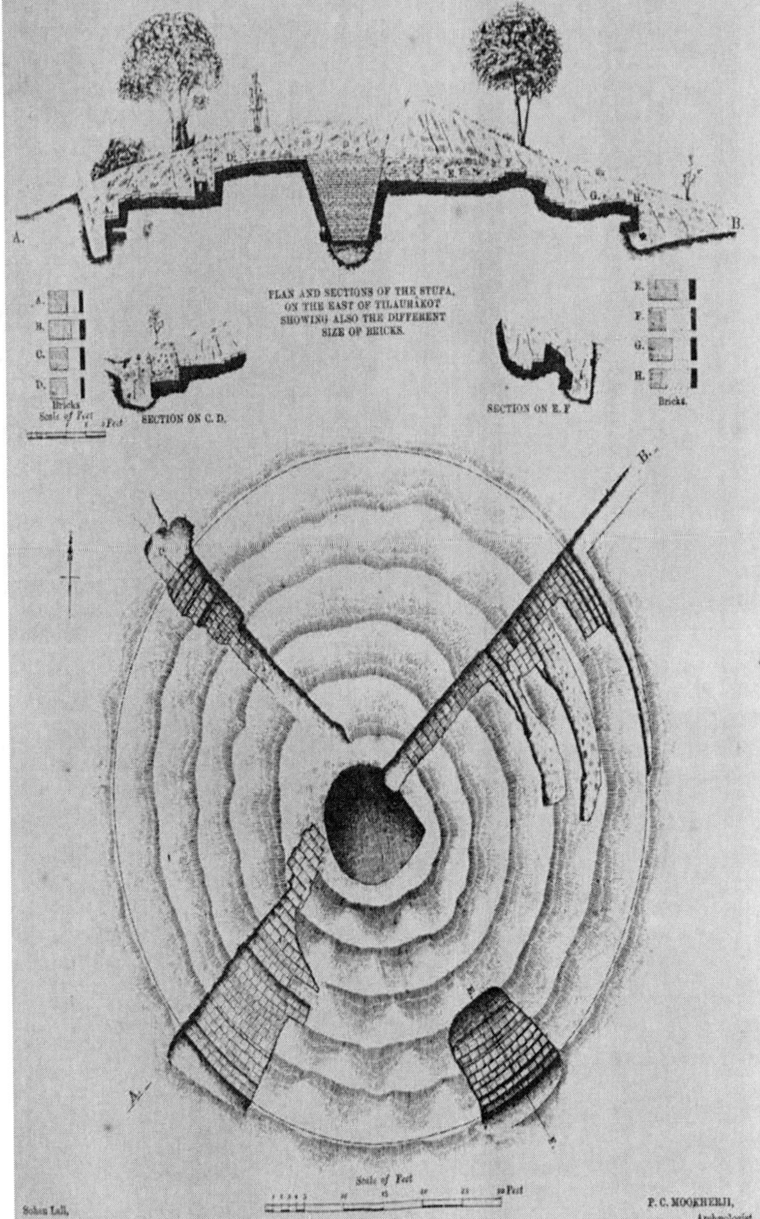

Sohan Lall,
Draftsman.

P. C. MOOKHERJI,
Archæologist.

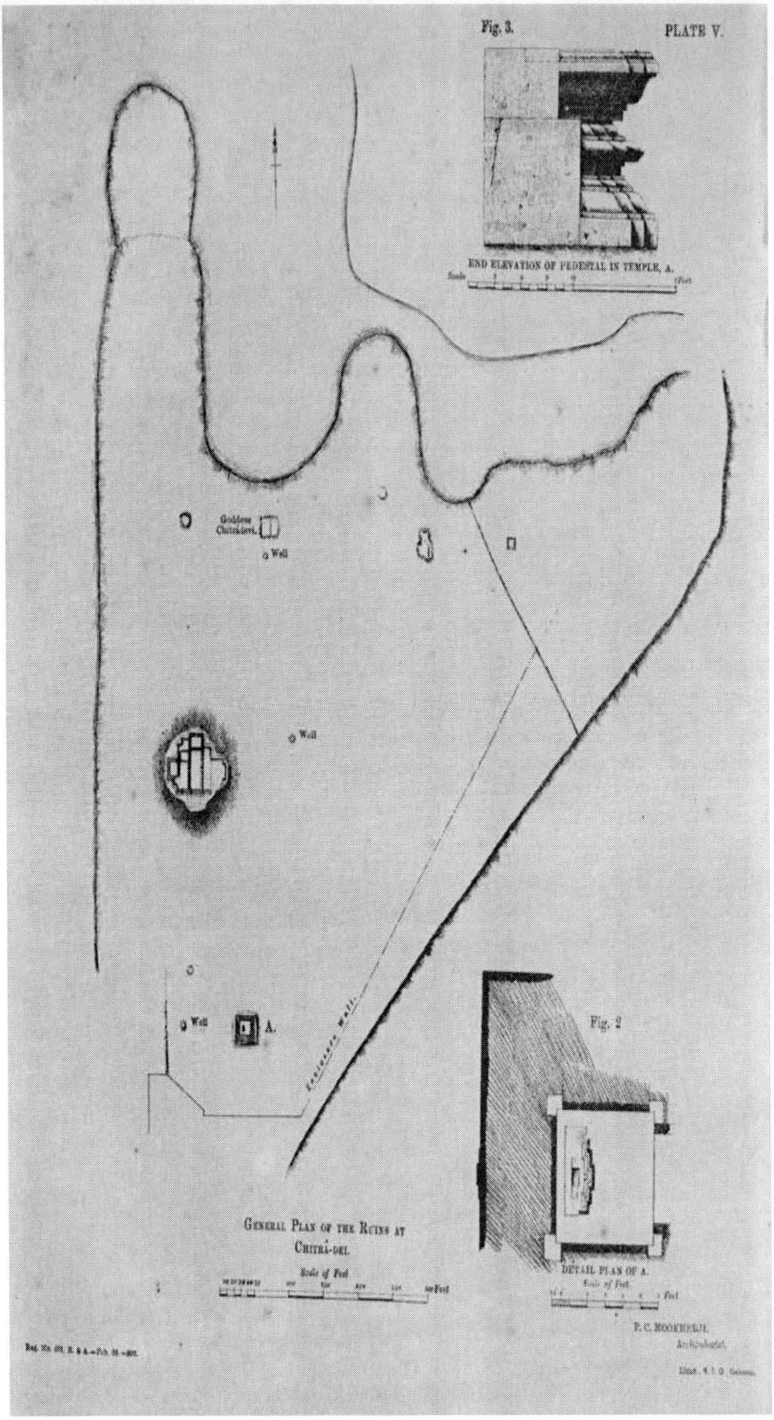
PLATE V.
Fig. 3.
END ELEVATION OF PEDESTAL IN TEMPLE, A.
Scale
Feet
Goddess Chitrâdevi.
Well
Well
Well
A.
Fig. 2
DETAIL PLAN OF A.
Scale of Feet.
Feet
GENERAL PLAN OF THE RUINS AT CHITRÂ-DEI.
Scale of Feet
Feet
P. C. MOOKHERJI,
Archæologist.

PLATE VI.

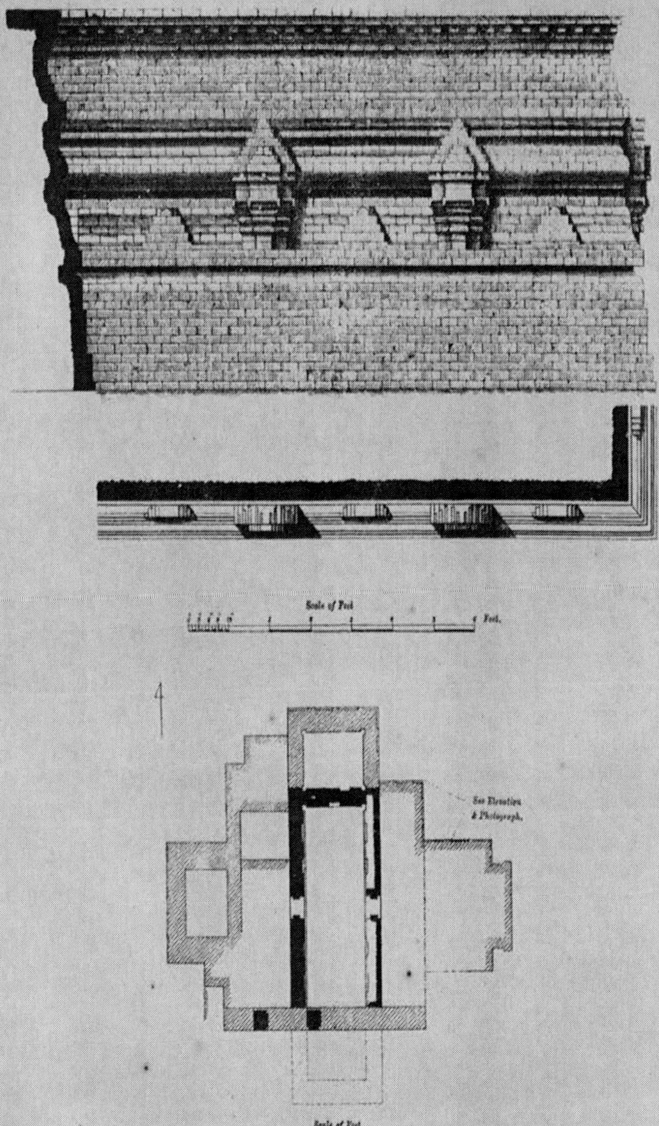

PLAN OF THE GREAT TEMPLE AND
PART-ELEVATION OF THE PLINTH,
CHITRÂ-DEI.

Sohan Lall,
Draftsman.

P. C. MOOKHERJI,
Archæologist.

Fig. 1. PLATE VII.

CHITIA-DEI. PLINTH OF THE GREAT TEMPLE, FROM N.E.

Fig. 2.

Photogravure. Survey of India Offices, Calcutta, December 1899.

RUMMIN-DEI. CARVED BRICKS.

P. C. Mukherji Archaeologist.

PLATE IX.

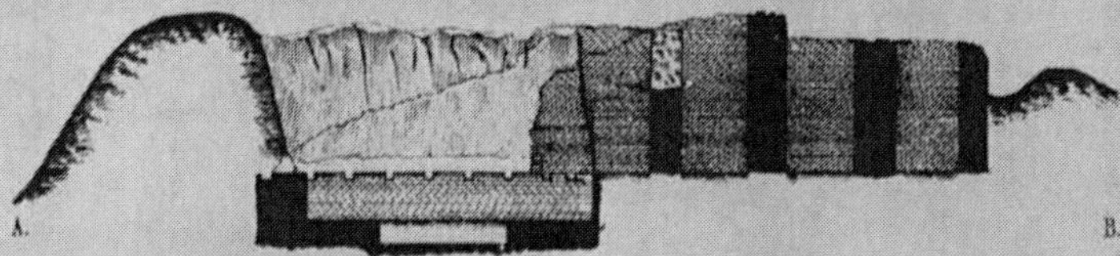

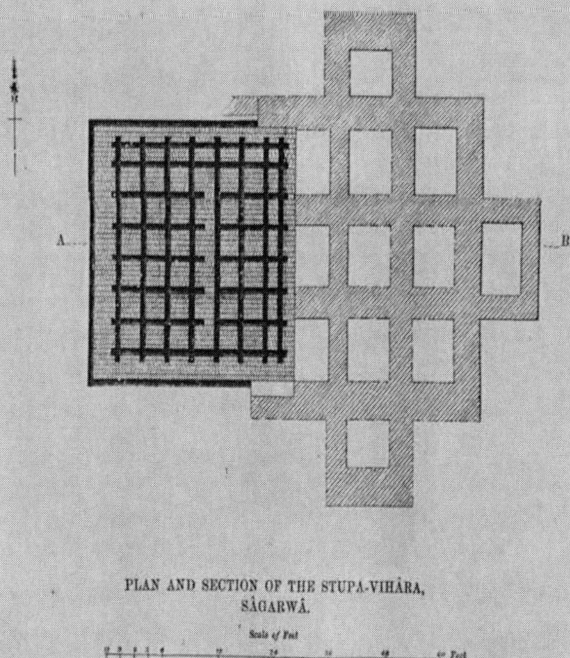

PLAN AND SECTION OF THE STUPA-VIHÂRA,
SÂGARWÂ.

Scale of Feet

Feet

Sohan Lall,
Draftsman.

P. C. MOOKHERJI,
Archæologist.

PLATE X.

Photogravure.

Survey of India Offices, Calcutta, December 189[illegible].

SAGARWA. GENERAL PLAN OF THE EXCAVATED RUINS, FROM WEST. (OR LOOKING EAST.)

Bhairava Buksh, Draftsman.

PLATE XI.

Fig. 1.

KEY-PLAN OF STUPA No. 6.

Scale of Feet.

10 Feet

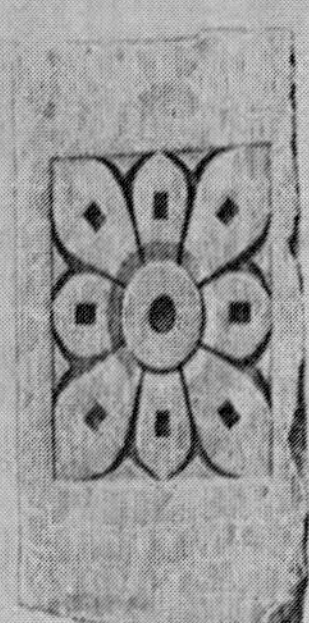

THE LAST BRICK, UNDER WHICH THE COPPER-CASKET WAS FOUND.

PLAN OF THE LOWEST LAYER OF BRICKS IN STUPA No. 6, SÁGARWÁ.

Scale of Feet.

Inches 12 9 6 3 0 1 *Foot*

Bhairwa Baksh,
Draftsman.

P. C. MOOKHERJI,
21-3-99. Archæologist.

PLATE XIa.

Fig. 2.

PLAN OF THE LOWEST LAYER OF BRICKS
IN STUPA No. 8.

Scale of Feet

KEY-PLAN OF STUPA No. 8.

Scale of Feet

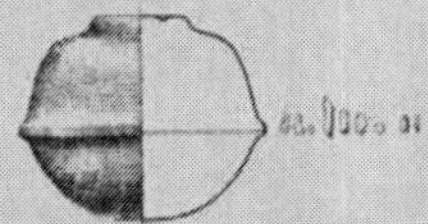

COPPER RELIC-CASKET, FOUND
UNDER THE CENTRAL BRICK.

Scale of Inches

NOTE.—This Plate, Figs. 1 & 2, was prepared under Dr. Fuhrer's supervision in 1898.

Bhairava Buksh,
Draftsman.

P. C. MOOKHERJI,
31-3-99. Archæologist.

PLATE XII.

Fig. 1.

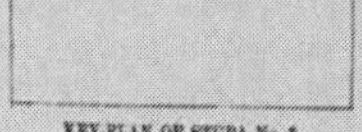

KEY-PLAN OF STUPA No. 9.

Scale of Feet.

PLAN OF THE LOWEST LAYER OF BRICKS
IN STUPA No. 9.

Scale of Feet

COPPER RELIC CASKET, FOUND
UNDER THE CENTRAL BRICK.

Scale of Inches

NOTE.—This Plate, Figs. 1 & 2, was prepared under
Dr. Führer's supervision in 1898.

Bhairon Baksh,
Draftsman.

P. C. MOOKHERJI,
21-3-98. Archæologist.

PLATE XIIa.

Fig. 2.

THE LOTUS-BRICK ABOVE THE CASKET.

THE LAYER ABOVE THE LOTUS.

NOTE.—This layer is drawn down-side up. Under the square Lotus-brick, was found a broken copper casket, with two gold Leaves.

KEY-PLAN OF STUPA No. 10.

Scale of Feet

PLAN OF THE THREE LOWEST LAYERS OF BRICKS, IN STUPA No. 10, SÂGARWÂ.

Inches — *Scale of Feet* — Feet

Bhawani Baksh, Draftsman.

P. C. MOOKHERJI, Archæologist.

21.3.99.

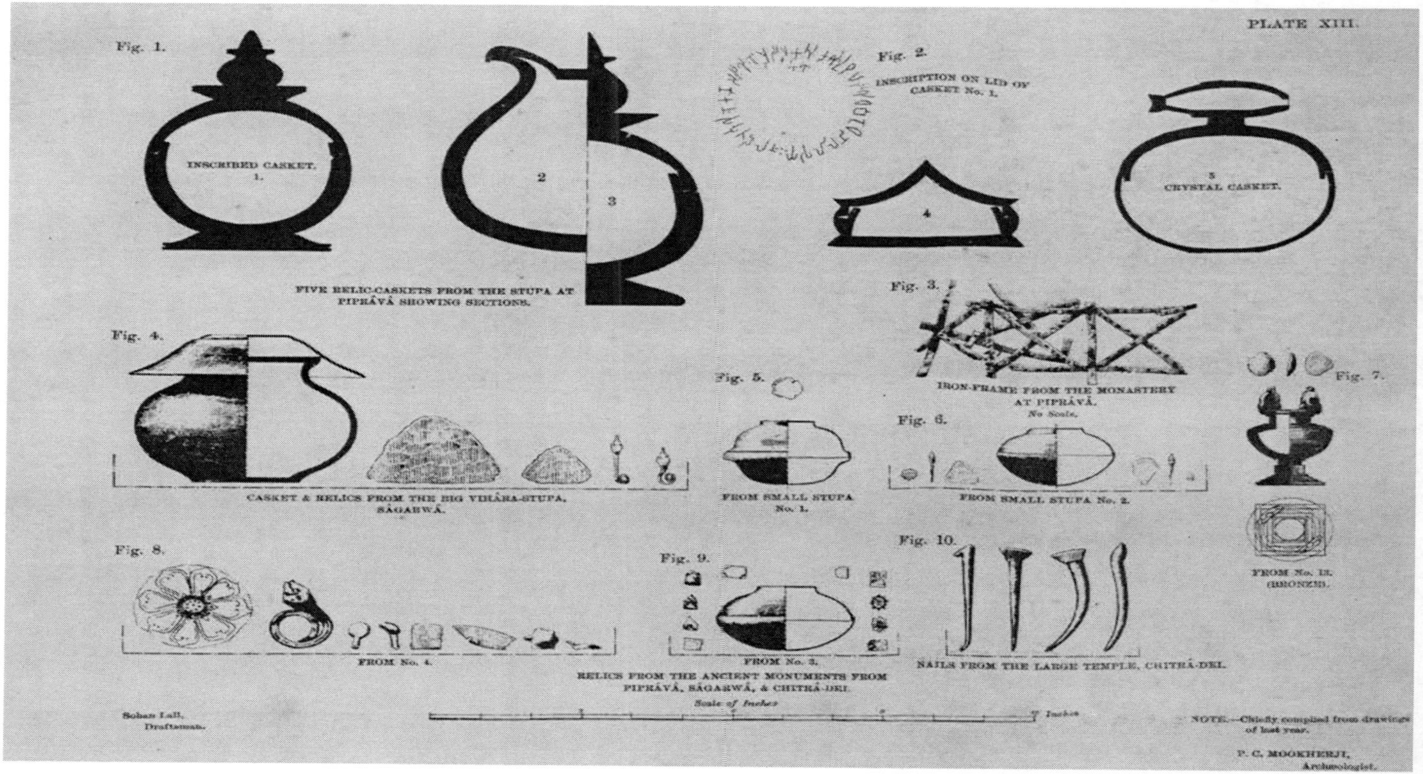
PLATE XIII.
Fig. 1.
INSCRIBED CASKET.
1.
2
3
Fig. 2.
INSCRIPTION ON LID OF
CASKET No. 1.
4
5
CRYSTAL CASKET.
FIVE RELIC-CASKETS FROM THE STUPA AT
PIPRÂVÂ SHOWING SECTIONS.
Fig. 3.
IRON-FRAME FROM THE MONASTERY
AT PIPRÂVÂ.
No Scale.
Fig. 4.
CASKET & RELICS FROM THE BIG VIHÂRA-STUPA,
SÂGARWÂ.
Fig. 5.
FROM SMALL STUPA
No. 1.
Fig. 6.
FROM SMALL STUPA No. 2.
Fig. 7.
FROM No. 11.
(BRONZE).
Fig. 8.
FROM No. 4.
Fig. 9.
FROM No. 3.
Fig. 10.
NAILS FROM THE LARGE TEMPLE, CHITRÂ-DEI.
RELICS FROM THE ANCIENT MONUMENTS FROM
PIPRÂVÂ, SÂGARWÂ, & CHITRÂ-DEI.
Scale of Inches
Inches
Sohan Lall,
Draftsman.
NOTE.—Chiefly compiled from drawings
of last year.
P. C. MOOKHERJI,
Archæologist.

PLATE XIV.

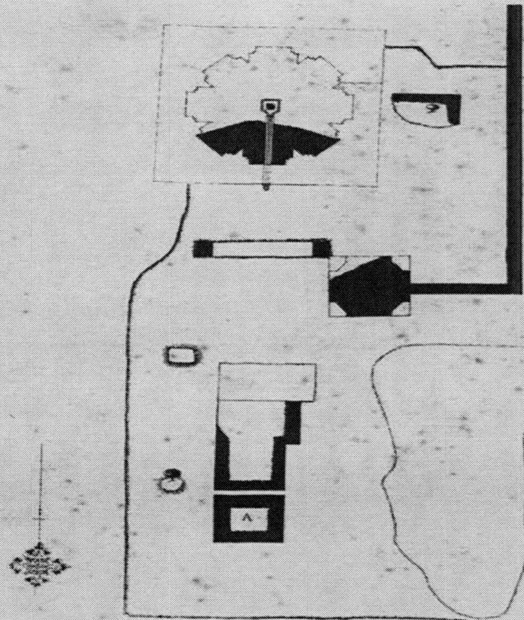

GENERAL PLAN OF THE RUINS
AT BIKULI.

Scale of Feet

Sohan Lall,
Draftsman.

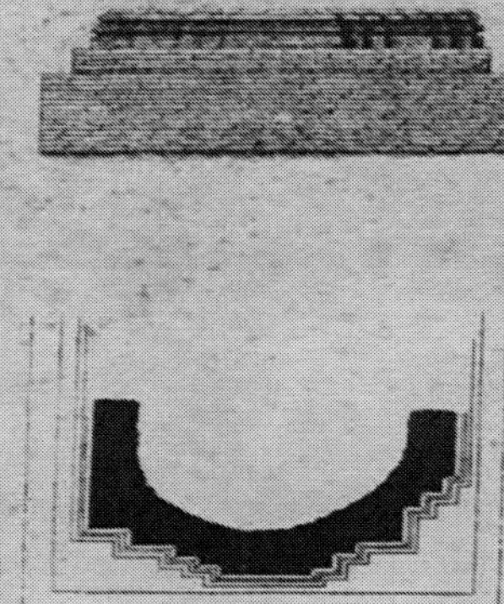

DETAIL-PLAN & BACK-ELEVATION OF
THE SMALL TEMPLE, MARKED A.

Scale of Feet

P. C. MOOKHERJI,
Archaeologist.

Fig. 1.

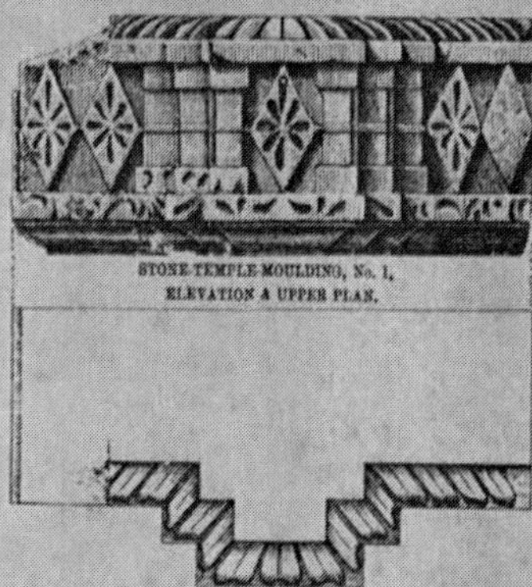

STONE-TEMPLE-MOULDING, No. 1,
ELEVATION & UPPER PLAN.

Fig. 2.

STONE-TEMPLE-MOULDING, No. 2.

Fig. 3.

CAPITAL OF A PILASTER, PLAN
& ELEVATIONS.

Fig. 4.

PART-ELEVATION & SECTION. HALF-PLAN.

LINGA & YONI.

RELICS AT BIKULI.

Scale of Feet

Inches 12 9 6 3 1 Foot.

Sohan Lall,
Draftsman.

P. C. MOOKHERJI,
Archæologist.

Fig. 5.

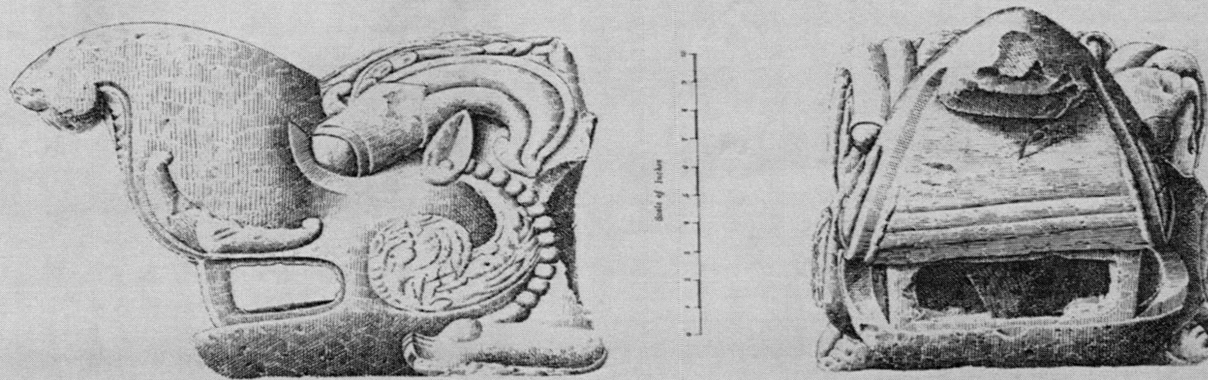

PROFILE. FRONT.

MOUTH-PIECE OF A DRAIN-PIPE OF A
TEMPLE, SIDE & FRONT.
BIKULI.

Bhairava Buksh,
Draftsman.

P. C. MOOKHERJI,
1899. Archæologist.

Fig. 1.

NIGÂLI PILLAR AT NIGLIVÂ
WITH PLAN & SECTION OF TOP.

Fig. 2.

THE PILLAR (PUTESVARA)
& CAPITAL AT GUTIVÂ
PLAN & ELEVATION.

Fig. 3.

CAPITAL OF THE PILLAR
AT RUMMIN-DEI.

Fig. 4.

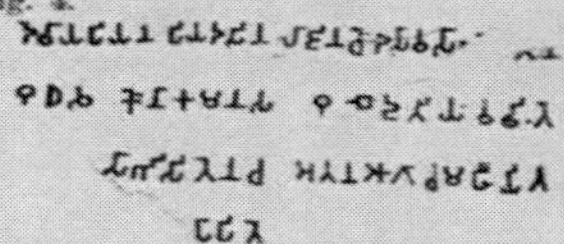

DETAIL OF THE NIGÂLI INSCRIPTION.
No Scale.

Scale of Feet

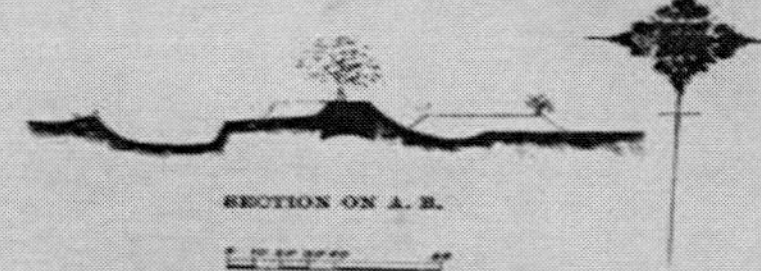

SECTION ON A. B.

Fig. 5.

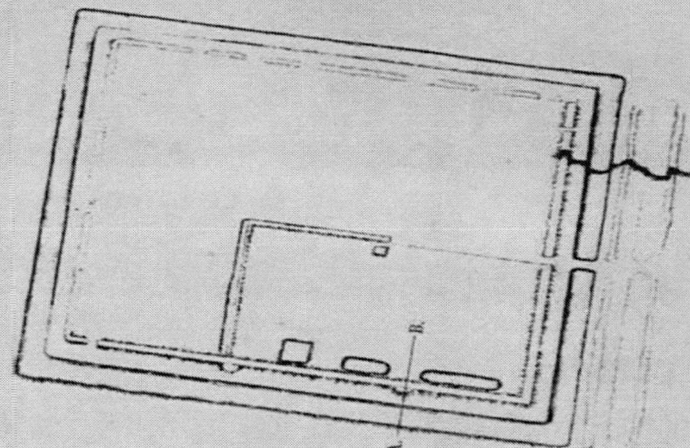

ROUGH PLAN OF THE KOT
AT ARAURÂ.

Scale of Feet

Sohan Lall,
Draftsman.

P. C. MOOKHERJI,
1899. Archæologist.

PLATE XVII.

Fig. 2.

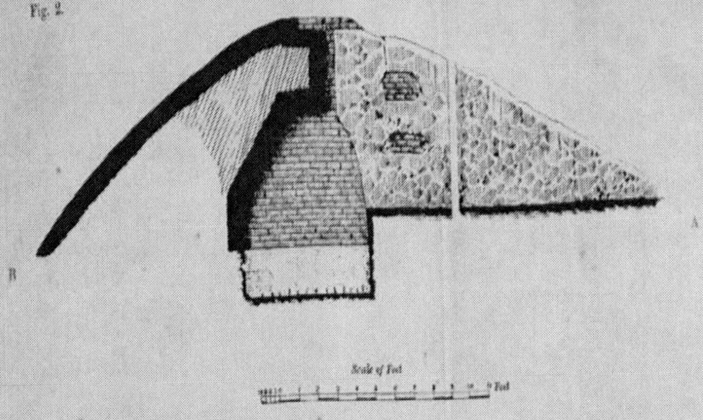

Fig. 1

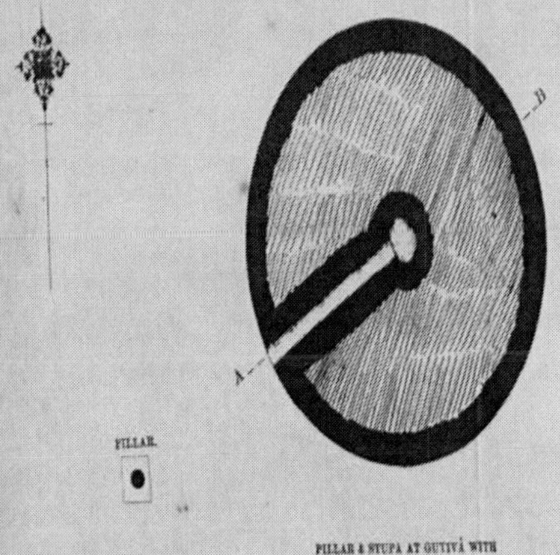

PILLAR & STUPA AT GUTIVÁ WITH SECTION OF THE LATTER.

Scale of Feet

Fig. 3.

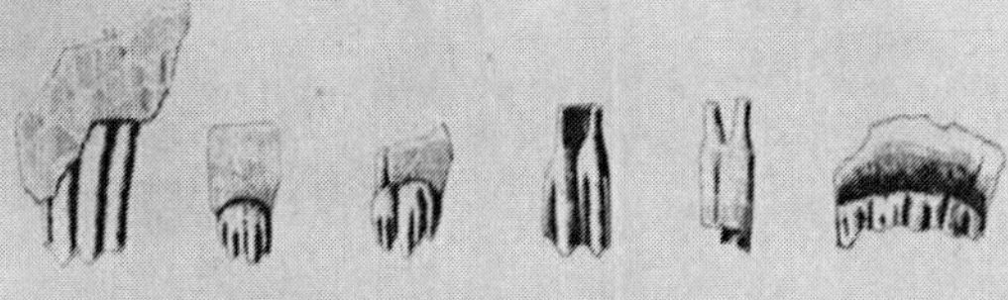

BONES (TEETH) FOUND IN THE STUPA.

Scale of Inches

Sohan Lal,
Draftsman.

P. C. MOOKHERJI,
Archæologist.

Fig. 1. PLATE XIX.

RUMMIN-DEI. VIEW OF THE RUINS FROM THE WEST.

Fig. 2.

Photogravure. Survey of India Offices Calcutta, December 1899.

RUMMIN-DEI. VIEW OF THE RUINS FROM THE SOUTH.

P. C. Mukherji, Archaeologist.

PLATE XX.

Fig. 1.

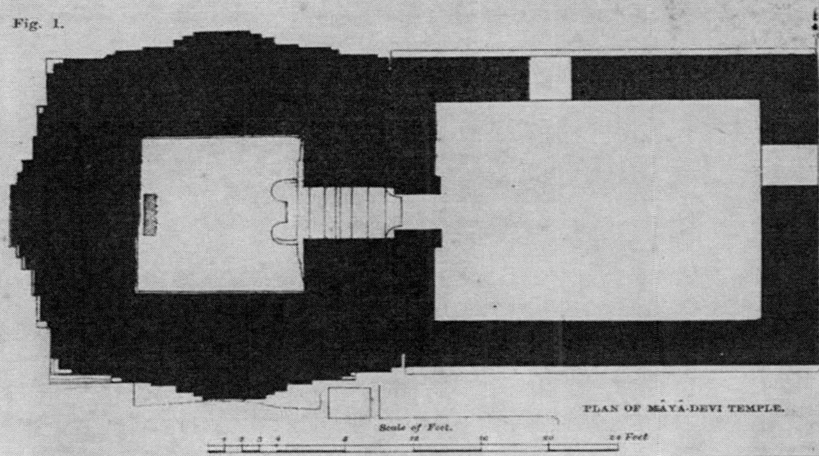

PLAN OF MĀYĀ-DEVI TEMPLE.

Fig 3.

Fig 2.

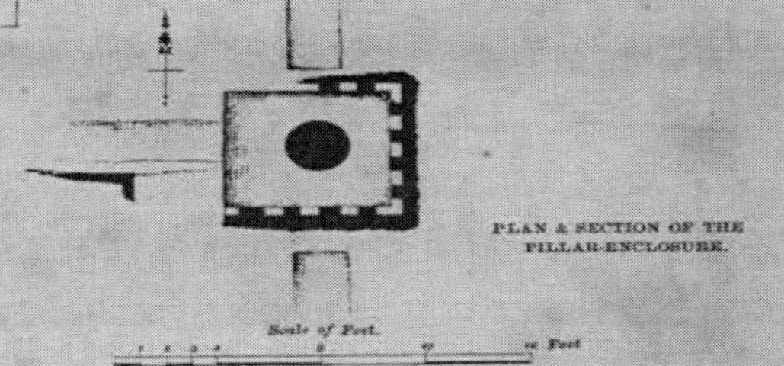

PLAN & SECTION OF THE PILLAR-ENCLOSURE.

Fig. 4.

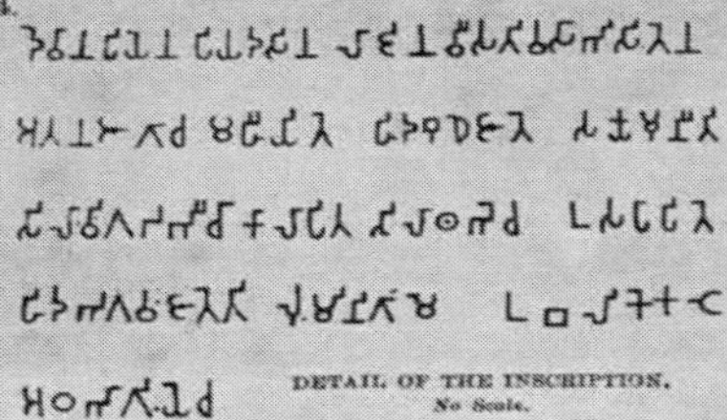

DETAIL OF THE INSCRIPTION.
No Scale.

Sohan Lall,
Draftsman.

P. C. MOOKHERJI,
Archæologist.

PLATE XXI.

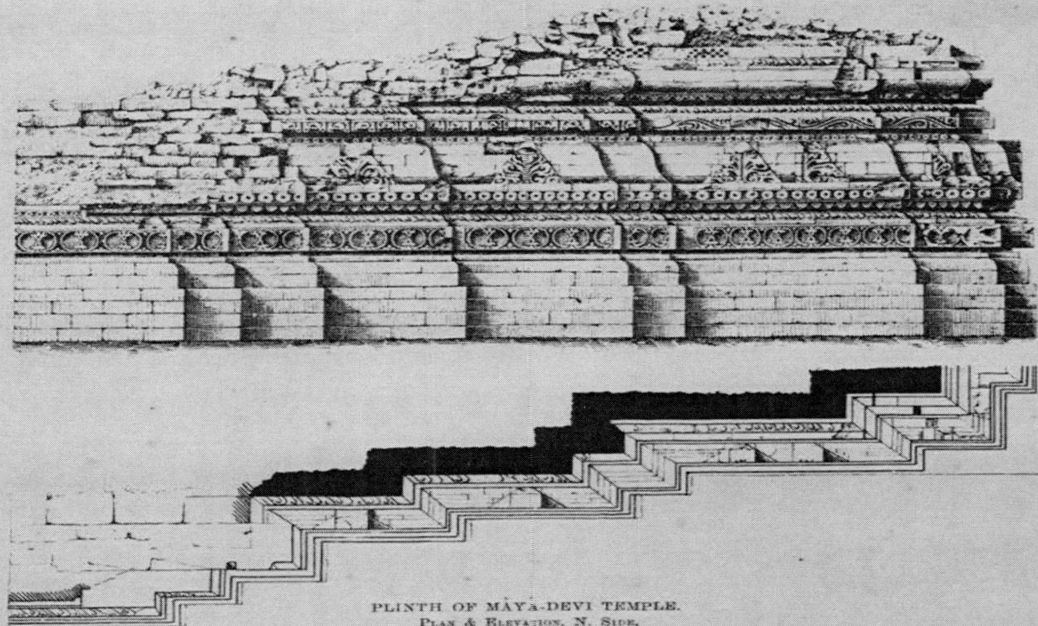

PLINTH OF MÂYÂ-DEVI TEMPLE.
PLAN & ELEVATION, N. SIDE,
Western Half.

Scale of Inches

Sohan Lall,
Draftsman.

P. C. MOOKHERJI,
Archæologist.

Fig. 1. PLATE XXII.

RUMMIN-DEI. VIEW OF MÂYÂ-DEVIÈS TEMPLE, SHOWING FOUR PERIODS OF BUILDINGS FROM S. W.

Fig. 2.

Photogravure. Survey of India Offices, Calcutta, December 1899.

ORNAMENTAL PLINTH OF THE TEMPLE, NORTH WEST CORNER.

P. C. Mukherji Archaeologist.

Fig. 1. PLATE XXIII

RUMMIN-DEI. SMALL STUPA, SOUTH WEST OF MÂYÂ-DEVI TEMPLE.

Fig. 2.

Photogravure

Survey of India Offices Calcutta, December 1899.

SMALL STUPA, SOUTH OF MÂYÂ-DEVI TEMPLE.

P. C. Mukherji Archaeologist.

Fig. 1.

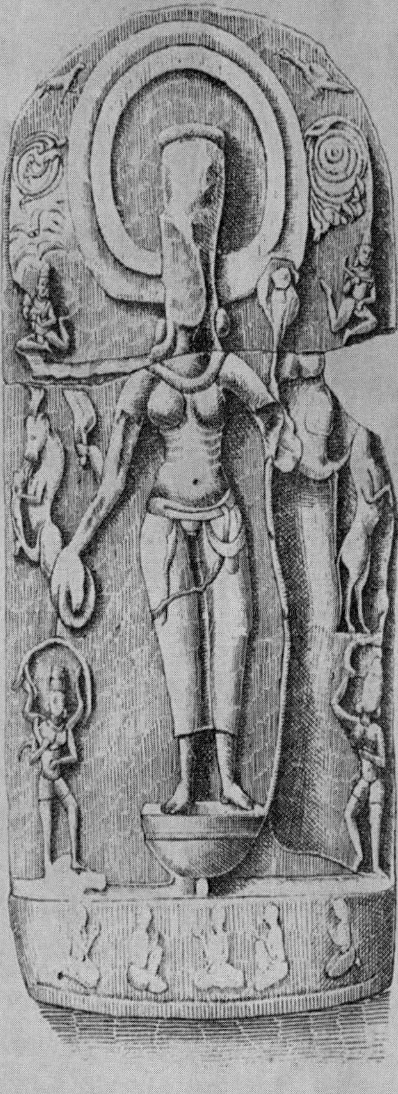

VÁRÁHI OR TÁRÁ-DEVI

Scale of Feet

P. C. MOOKHERJI,
18-3-99. Archæologist.

PLATE XXIVa.

Fig. 2.

MÂYÂ-DEVI.

Scale of Feet

Inches 12 8 6 4 2 0 1 2 Feet

P. C. MOOKHERJI,

18.3.99. Archæologist.

PLATE XXV.

Fig. 1.

TWO PEDESTALS OF TEMPLE-STATUES.

Fig. 2.

Fig. 3.

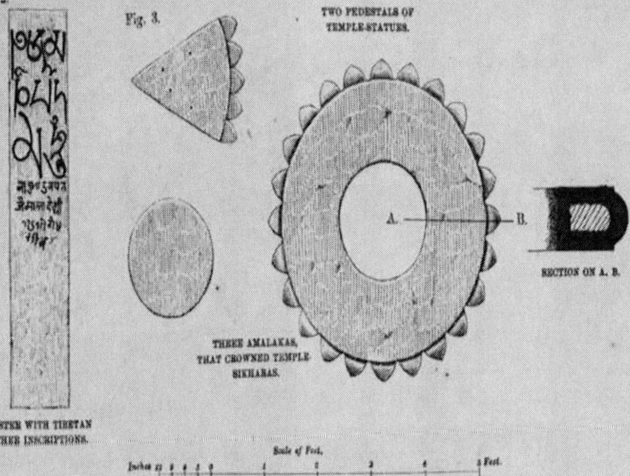

PILASTER WITH TIBETAN & OTHER INSCRIPTIONS.

THREE AMALAKAS, THAT CROWNED TEMPLE SIKHARAS.

Fig. 4.

Fig. 5.

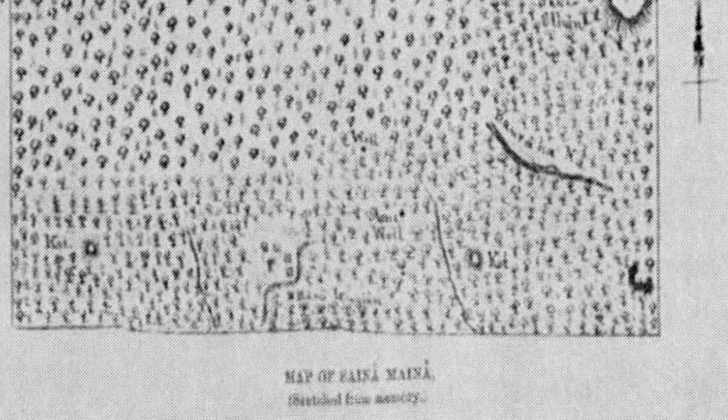

Sohan Lall,
Draftsman.

MAP OF RAINĀ MAINĀ.
(Sketched from memory.)

P. C. MOOKHERJI,
Archaeologist.

Fig. 1.

TWO PEDESTALS OF PILLARS OF MÂYA-DEVI TEMPLE.

Scale of Feet.

Inches 9 6 3 0 1 2 Feet

Fig. 2.

1. TERRA-COTTA BUDDHA.

2. HEAD OF BUDDHA.

3. PADMAPÂNI.

SIX RELICS AT RUMMIN-DEI.

No Scale.

4. TÂRÂ.

5. PÂRVATI OF A GAURI-SANKAR-GROUP.

6. LOWER PIECE OF JAMB OF A SCULPTURED DOOR.

Fig 3.

DURGÂ AT BARI SISANIÂ.

Fig. 4.

SCULPTURED DOOR DOHNI.

Restored.

Scale of Feet.

Inches 12 9 6 3 0 1 2 Feet

Sohan Lall, Draftsman.

P. C. MOOKHERJI, Archæologist.

PLATE XXVII.

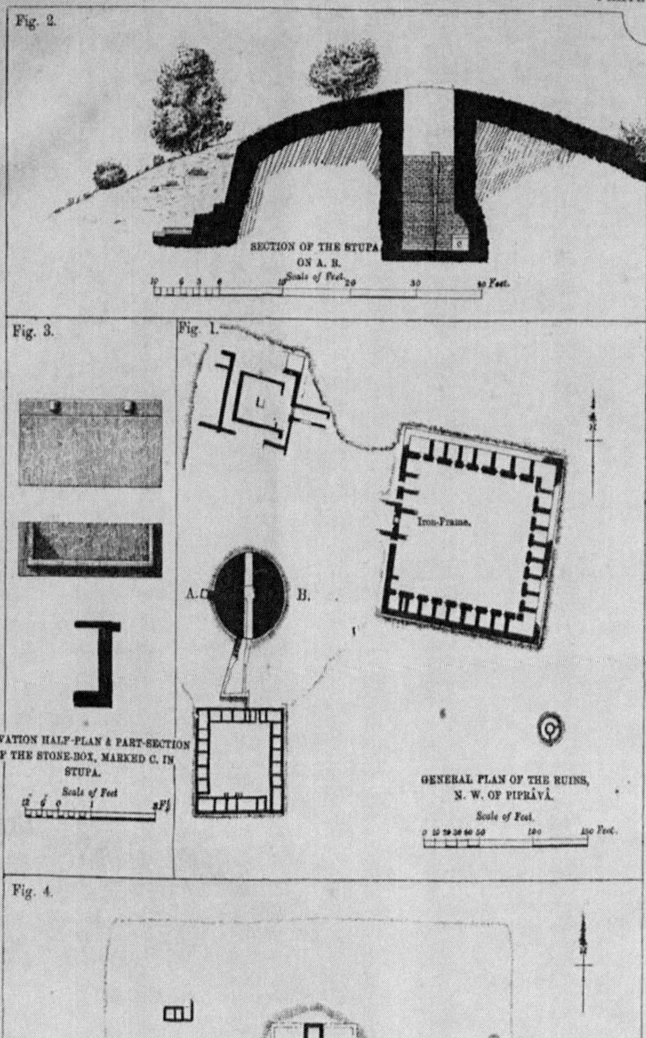

Sohan Lall,
Draftsman.

P. C. MOOKHERJI,
Archaeologist.

Fig. 1. PLATE XXVIII.

PIPRÂVÂ. VIEW OF THE STUPA, SO FAR AS EXHUMED, FROM SOUTH.

Fig. 2.

Photogravure. Survey of India Offices, Calcutta, December 18[illegible]

FIVE RELIC CASKETS FROM THE STONE BOX FROM THE STUPA.

P. C. Mukherji, Archaeologist.